Acknow

Special thanks to African Mami and our fellow Adventurers for believing that this was possible, and to Caroline, for making it so.

To Ciara,

Such a pleasure to meet you! I hope you enjoy this literary ride!

—Malaka

The black cock that patrolled the compound crowed at 4 am. The pompous fowl's throaty, urgent appeal for the masses to start the day was one of the things that Afosua found endearing about being back home. Still, being so ungraciously jarred from sleep was an annoyance she could do without. Why did her rooster have to be an over-achiever? Why couldn't he be more like the other neighborhood roosters and crow at 5 o'clock instead? On any other day she would have resented the yard bird for sounding his rousing alarm so early in the morning and although she was rankled today, she was grateful for it. There were many things she needed to accomplish that day, the first being to get the stranger out of her bed. In the pre-dawn light, she made out the shape of a man's back rising and falling rhythmically as he slept. He was broad and muscular – a magnificent sight to behold – but he still had to get out of her house.

"Hey," Afosua said, shaking him gently at first.

He slept on.

"Hey!" she whispered louder.

"Mmmm?"

"It's time to get up."

She had already slipped into her morning coat and was belting it as she spoke. She switched on the water heater and went to her closet to pull out her suit for work. At 32, Afosua was the youngest manager at Phillips & Boakye, a start-up firm located in Cantonments. It was a niche company in the financial field in Ghana, providing actuary services and data analysis to both government and private entities. It was work that required travel into both the hallowed halls of parliament and the most remote parts of Ghana. It was considered 'man's work' – not because of its complexity but because of the exclusivity of it. Business deals were made over beer in private mansions and government back offices... hardly appropriate places for a young Ghanaian woman to be seen or to be rumored to have been seen.

Although new to the field, Phillips & Boakye had a strong reputation in the financial world. That was because of the care with which they handled their clients' information. With so much at stake there was no room for error at this stage in the game, and being the only woman in management left Afosua even less room for oversight.

Her thoughts soon shifted from her new job. Annoyed, she noted that the man in her bed had not yet woken up. She ripped the sheets off him and stood over him.

"Seriously, it's time to get up. I have to go to work, and I presume you do too."

This was always the hard part about picking up guys. They never seemed to recognize when the welcome mat had been snatched from under their feet.

"But the sun's not even up yet!" he objected groggily, reaching for the sheet to re-cover himself.

"I know. All the more reason for you to get a move on," she said sweetly. "We wouldn't want you to encounter my father, would we?"

That made the man sit straight up.

"Yes. Yes you're right...of course!"

He grabbed his trousers from the floor and quickly went to wash his face. Afosua listened to him splash noisily as the gardener began sweeping fallen mango leaves in the courtyard. The sound of the gardener's stiff broom scratching concrete blended with the same dirge he had hummed every morning since he had begun working for her family ten years ago. The whole house would be stirring with activity in the next hour.

Afosua sighed.

It pained her that she had to resort to evoking the name of her father to get this man's attention – whatever his name was – but it seemed to be the only thing that local men ever responded to. Her father had died two years ago. Unless he was afraid of ghosts, Mr. Stranger had nothing to fear of a dead man. Now her mother! That was an entirely different story.

Whatever the case, a gentleman should leave when asked to, at the first request.

Afosua jumped into the shower, not bothering to wait for the water to heat up completely. Getting him out of the house was far more important than her comfort at this point. With any luck, he would just leave and get himself a taxi. Luck, it seemed, had abandoned her. After Afosua emerged from the bathroom, she saw her guest waiting for her by the door.

"Could I get a lift into town?" he asked sheepishly.

"I can take you as far as the junction," she assured him.

"Which way are you going?"

"Not the direction you're going in, I can promise you that."

The man seemed wounded by her cold response. She backtracked a little, not wanting to seem too hard. She offered him a tight smile.

"Come on. We'll stop by the bakery and get a cinnamon roll on the way."

The pair rode in virtual silence until they got to Auntie Aggie's Bakery. This was the part about the morning-after that Afosua disliked most: the awkward silence shared with a perfect stranger. The silence which threatened to suffocate them both as they grappled for something meaningful to say. What kind of small talk does one have with someone whose name you don't even know? She could tell him anything he might want to know about the night before. How he'd made her body quiver in ways she'd never imagined possible. How the taste of his sweat was delightful and tangy on her tongue. How excited she was at that moment, thinking about the few hours they'd just shared. She could tell him anything he wanted to know about himself... except his name, because it didn't matter.

Afosua was happy that Auntie Aggie's was close by. Breakfast not only created a diversion, but eating at Aggie's also made her feel like she was doing a good deed. Afosua patronized Aggie because she was a self-made woman who had survived a hard life by the sheer use of her wits. A product of an old but enduring culture that didn't see the value in educating girls, Auntie Aggie had taken the brave step of going to remedial classes and learning to read after the age of 50. For that she had earned Afosua's eternal respect – and her gratitude for making such delicious pastries. Afosua honked her horn and waited for the overweight but surprisingly spritely woman to emerge from behind the glass counter, where Aggie was directing her assistant to place a fresh batch of pies. Auntie Aggie flashed a broad grin.

"Eiii! Afos. Fine morning!" Auntie Aggie greeted her warmly.

She gave the man in the car a saucy look.

"And who is this your friend?"

Afosua shifted her weight in the driver's seat and frowned as she opened the car door. Auntie Aggie was an experienced woman of the world. She knew Afosua didn't know anything about him, just like the other men she'd brought by for breakfast before. This was the older woman's cloaked way of scolding her. Fortunately, Auntie Aggie was focused more on feeding than heckling her that morning. She pointed excitedly to her new glass counter.

"What do you want this morning? I have so many nice pastries!" she gushed. "And you can see them so nice now that I have this fine glass to put it behind."

Afosua looked over at Mr. Stranger, who was smiling at the large woman cheerfully waving her hands over her wares. No doubt that this is how he liked to be greeted in the morning – with a broad bosom and something hot to eat placed in front of his face. Afosua was not the sort to fuss over a man, which is exactly why she brought all her dates to see Aggie, no matter how untoward it might appear to the older woman. The pair thanked Aggie after they made their purchases and returned to the car. Afosua stopped the man before he could get in.

"The junction is just over there." Afosua slid into the driver's seat and nodded towards the end of the road.

Mr. Stranger smiled wryly.

"I had a good time last night," he said sincerely.

"So did I."

She refused to meet his eyes. She didn't want to see the begging look that came with the morning after. It was so exhausting.

"Maybe I'll see you soon?" He sounded hopeful.

She smiled and sparked her engine without offering confirmation or denial. The treatment she was giving this man was precisely why they came home with *her* and not the other way round. She'd learned the hard way from her past mistakes. Still, she could afford a bit of cordiality.

"Have a great day..."

"Tony. The name's Tony. You have a good day too, Afosua."

She looked at Tony from her rearview mirror as she drove off. What would make such a sweet man come home with her on a whim? The men she picked up were usually assholes who couldn't be bothered to remember her name. All they ever wanted was a quick lay, and she was happy to oblige as long as there were no feelings, hurt or otherwise involved.

Tony's name rolled around in her mind for longer than she wanted. She shook her head and focused on weaving her way through Accra traffic. It was going to be a hectic day at work.

******

Afosua was not a stunning woman but she was difficult to ignore. At 5'9" she stood taller than most women and eye to eye to most men. Her skin was mahogany brown with red undertones, and her eyes were the color of coal. They were cool and piercing, as if mechanically analyzing everything she surveyed. There was an enigma about her that made people either want to get to know her better or shy away completely. That was the way it was with her: all or nothing.

When she walked into the office, the receptionist greeted her warmly.

"Good morning, Ms. Gyemfi!" she chirped.

"Good morning, Gertrude," Afosua returned. "Where are the big guys?"

Afosua looked towards Mark Phillips' and Harold Boakye's office doors. Both were shut, indicating that they were either not in or not to be disturbed.

"They've met with the Swedes this morning," Gertrude replied uneasily.

Afosua was miffed. She had been excluded again. When she joined Phillips & Boakye six months before, she had been hired into management, wooed with the promise of being a part of key decisions with important clients. So far, she had been left out of almost every major conference, and she knew exactly why. While Mark Phillips was the brains behind the company, Harold Boakye held the purse strings. The only son and heir of a gold baron, it was his financial support that kept the company in the black while it built its base. Both men had been friends since their secondary school days at Achimota, and were in their late 40s.

Their age provided them every advantage. In a culture that correlated age with respect, they had the benefit of commanding it without question but were still young enough to be persuaded by reason and new ideas. However, one of these fellows had somehow managed not to change his archaic views about the role of women.

That person was Harold Boakye.

While Mark welcomed Afosua as a valued addition to the team, Harold resented her very presence at the bargaining table. Whatever their positions or ideas about women, neither man could deny that she was a brilliant analyst. This is why they presented all their findings and data to Afosua after every meeting with a client.

"Alright then," Afosua sighed. "I'll wait till they get back. Thank you Gertrude."

"You're welcome, Ms. Gyemfi."

Afosua shot the receptionist a side glance, remembering when things were not so cozy between the two of them. Before Afosua joined the company, Gertrude was the only female employee and had become accustomed to the undivided attention of every man in the office. She had seen Afosua's arrival as a direct threat to that attention.

Gertrude had wanted to let Afosua know exactly how she felt about having another woman in her office. She welcomed Afosua by turning in her reports late, dropping her calls and serving her cold coffee. Being older, Afosua quickly saw past these childish antics and addressed Gertrude's insecurity by taking her to lunch one day. Gertrude mistook the invitation as a meek acknowledgement of *her* authority. Nothing in Afosua's demeanor that day confirmed that assumption. Her eyes held Gertrude's in a cold, hard stare for the duration of their meal.

"Let's be friends, okay? I can be a wonderful friend or an even more formidable enemy," Afosua cautioned the recent university graduate. "Your best bet is to make me your friend."

Things got better soon after that.

Afosua threw her purse onto the red leather wingback chair in her office and blew out a loud, frustrated breath. She picked up a pair of black digital dice that a friend had given her for her birthday and blew on them before rolling them on the table. If you asked them any question, they were supposed to predict the outcome accurately.

"Will I have a good day at work today?" she asked the dice.

"No," came the mechanical reply.

"Oh. Will I have a better day than yesterday?"

She rolled the dice again.

"No."

"Well fuck me!" she blurted. Why should she believe this hunk of digitized plastic anyway?

"I'd be happy to!"

Afosua whipped around and saw Robert Acquah's broad frame filling out the door to her office. She was overpowered by the scent of turmeric and allspice, undertones of the expensive cologne that he had applied much too liberally for this early in the morning.

"Good morning, Robert."

"Good morning, Afosua," he purred, moving in a little closer.

Afosua stepped away from him and sat behind her desk, powering up her desktop. She would have welcomed his advances under normal circumstances, just as she had done the first week she began working for Phillips & Boakye. Robert was an attractive man and reeked of sex. Hooking up with him was just the kind of welcome Afosua needed when she joined the firm. Even the discovery that he was engaged with a baby on the way did not deter her interest in him. However, the discovery that he was coupling with Gertrude (in the supply closet no less!) at the same time had made him irrevocably undesirable. Afosua could not tolerate the idea of sleeping with her subordinate who was in turn sleeping with *another* subordinate. It was just grotesque! She had abruptly ended their flirtation and had been enduring his tiresome attempts to reconnect ever since.

"I hear the bosses are out meeting with the Swedes this morning," she said in measured tones.

11

"Yes," confirmed Robert. "I met them walking out for together for breakfast as I came in."

"I should have been in on it," she mused.

"I'd like to get in *you*," Robert quipped wickedly, trailing his hand on the cuff of her sleeve.

Afosua was in no mood for this foolishness. She snatched her hand away.

"Look, I've got some work to do," she said dismissively. "When you've had a chance to take a look at that video, can you let me know what your observations are?"

He gave her a pained look as she recoiled so violently from him. She returned his expression with raised, expectant eyebrows, signaling that it was time to leave.

"Yes, madam!" he smirked.

Robert had sense enough to know when he wasn't wanted around, and went in search of easier prey. Afosua heard Gertrude giggling soon after he had left her office.

"Sooner rather than later, Robert," she called curtly.

She heard his footsteps retreating on the terrazzo floor and into the multi-media room.

No one knew it, but one of the reasons Phillips & Boakye was such a successful actuary service was because of the technology they used. It was simple, but very effective: hidden cameras. Ghana's voyeurism laws were so lax that they may as well not exist. Whenever there was a sales call, the entire meeting was recorded and analyzed later. Robert was an oversexed chauvinistic maniac, but no one was better at reading non-verbal cues than he was. Just by observing a client's body language, he could interpret what their mouth might not be admitting. He could assess sincerity, deception and fear. His findings were paired with the results of all the empirical data collected for any deal, and a benefit/risk analysis was provided for any proposed project. Phillip & Boakye understood what too few other actuaries in Ghana did: Numbers don't lie, but people do.

Afosua used the next four hours to answer emails and re-read the massive behavioral analysis report for the Swedes. Something didn't add up. In typical deals, a foreign firm swooped in to consume the lion's share of a project and left government middlemen with the scraps to fight over - that was standard practice in a country given over to corruption. The problem was she couldn't find any scraps at all.

The chime of her Blackberry shook her from her thoughts. It was Naa Akweley.

"Shit."

Afosua grabbed her purse and shuffled towards the door, her three-inch heels impeding her speed.

"Gertrude, take any messages that come in for me and leave them on my desk will you please?"

"Yes, of course." Gertrude barely looked up from her screen. She was probably chatting with someone on Facebook.

Afosua ducked her head into the office and shouted one more order.

"And stay out of the broom closet!"

Every relationship has its risks and its benefits. The key to having a successful relationship is learning to nurture the benefits so that they dwarf the risks, or eliminating the relationship completely if its risks prove to be lethal. Afosua was in the nurturing stage with Naa Akweley Blankson, but she had admitted to herself a while ago that she was looking forward to terminating their acquaintance when the time was right.

As she strode purposely to their reserved table at Maquis Tante Marie Restaurant in Labone, she was greeted by Naa Akweley's scowling face. Annette Prah was sitting with her, looking equally grim.

"You're late," scolded Naa Akweley.

"Yes...Sorry", Afosua conceded in mock apology. "I am indeed 8 minutes late."

She was not in the mood to give an explanation, and she was certain that Naa Akweley would dismiss it anyway. Naa Akweley was a striking woman, with full lips and a queenly air, but she also possessed one quality that made her a hideous human being. While Afosua admitted that she herself was hard, curt and maybe unreasonable at times, Naa Akweley harbored a character flaw that made her even more insufferable: she was completely unforgiving and without contrition.

Afosua gave her table mate a once-over before sitting down. She certainly looked the part of a pastor's wife. Not a strand of her shoulder-length mane was out of place and if one attempted to usurp another's rank, Naa Akweley would have easily frowned it into obedience. She wore a conservative but fashionable A-line dress that flattered her curves and accented her growing belly. Naa Akweley was four months pregnant. Maybe that's why she was more surly than usual these days. Perhaps the evil cow was just hungry!

When Afosua was seated, Annette brightened immediately.

"How are you darling?" she asked sweetly.

"I'm well!" smiled Afosua.

She squeezed her friend's hand. Afosua had known Annette for over 16 years, making her one of her closest friends. They'd met in boarding school and kept in touch even after Afosua left to study in England. Afosua might have considered Annette her best friend, if not for one thing: the woman was afflicted with odious levels of self-doubt. Afosua abhorred women without confidence, and despite all Annette's airs, Afosua could sniff out her insecurity. Annette wielded so much power and influence and yet she hardly knew what to do with them! Fortunately, Afosua DID know what to do with such gifts. Annette was a valuable ally who she needed to keep in her corner. That was why their friendship had endured.

It was Annette who had introduced Afosua to Naa Akweley, who was the wife of the powerful Pastor Ian Blankson. And it was Naa Akweley who was going to get Afosua what she needed – whether she knew it or not.

"I saw you at New Spirit's benefit dinner last night," said Annette girlishly. "Who was that hot guy you were stringing along?"

Afosua smiled mysteriously.

"Well...he's an accountant, and his name is..."

"Tony," interjected Naa Akweley harshly. "His name is Tony and he's our church's accountant."

She took a sip from her sparkling water before continuing. She scowled at the glass, as though the liquid were burning her lips. She motioned for the waiter to come over and instructed him to bring her another drink.

"I saw the two of you leave together," she continued.

Afosua felt a stone drop in her stomach. Under normal circumstances, she could care less who knew whom she slept with – but when that knowledge interfered with her business plans, that was problematic. Tony's now apparent affiliation with the church was a little closer than she cared for. Afosua chose her words carefully before she spoke.

"Yes, his name is Tony. He's a very sweet guy. Very nice."

Naa Akweley sucked her teeth softly and impatiently called for another waiter to come over.

"If we're done discussing your sex life perhaps we can order now," she barked.

Annette looked at Afosua and smiled sheepishly. She returned the gesture and tilted her head, silently telling Annette that it was alright. She could handle Naa Akweley herself.

While they waited for their meal to arrive, Afosua launched into her reason for asking the two ladies to lunch.

"I'd like the two of you to join me in Dumbai for a weekend getaway."

"Dumbai?" asked a surprised Annette. "Where the hell is that?"

Naa Akweley shot her a look. She did not approve of coarse language.

"It's northeast of here, near Kete-Krachi, just above Lake Volta." Afosua pulled out her iPad. "I've been twice before, and it totally rejuvenated me. I think every woman in Ghana should visit it if she has the chance. I'd like to share it with the two of you."

Annette brightened immediately. She loved to travel. She very rarely got the opportunity.

"Well you can count me in! I'm all up for recharging my system. Life in the city can be such a drain."

Naa Akweley wasn't so quickly sold. She couldn't figure out what Afosua was up to, but she knew the woman wanted *something* from her. Everyone did. She was instantly angered by the very *possibility* of being used, even if she had no proof. Her rebuke was swift.

"I can't believe you would even think to ask me to travel so close to my due date," she said with disdain. "You know how the roads are in this country. My husband wouldn't even hear of it!"

"I thought about that, and I thought we might hire a private aircraft to get us there," Afosua replied. "It would be quicker and easier than driving."

Naa Akweley hissed at her, slitting her almond shaped eyes.

"You don't know a thing about child birth, do you?" she asked condescendingly. She rubbed her full belly protectively. "That altitude at this stage in a pregnancy would cause early labor. But then, how could you know? You're just a single woman with no responsibilities, sleeping her way through life!"

Annette drew a sharp breath in dismay. Afosua was not fazed. She had endured stronger and cheaper shots than this one. She could take it, but she could also give it.

"Yes well, someone's got to keep people like your husband in business, don't they? I'm the woman he preaches about every Sunday. The 'lost soul'...you know, the one who 'needs saving.' I keep the offering buckets full of cash. By 'sleeping my way through life' I paid for that car you're driving and that dress you're wearing."

Annette grabbed Afosua's hand to try and calm her down. Afosua wrestled out of her grasp and leaned in a little closer to Naa Akweley, whispering her next words. "Without me, you'd be *nothing*."

She grabbed her purse and tossed ₵100 on the table before sauntering off without looking back.

"Have a great day ladies."

******

With lunch cut short so abruptly, Naa Akweley decided to go straight home. Her husband would not believe the gall of Afosua! She called for the maid to get her bags out of the car as she pulled into the driveway.

"Stella! Stella, where are you?"

Few things aggravated her more than when the maid did not come immediately when called for. Naa Akweley walked around the bottom of her expansive home in search of the help. Stella was not in the kitchen, nor was she in the laundry room. Perhaps she was cleaning the bathrooms upstairs. Naa Akweley went to look for her there... but froze when her foot touched the first stair. She heard a familiar sound and immediately felt ill.

The wooden slats on her bed were grating violently and she became acutely aware that her husband was fucking the maid – again.

She stood petrified in place, with one foot on the bottom stair and one hand on the banister. She felt like Lot's wife, trapped by her past and encased in an impenetrable crust of salty hatred. She couldn't breathe. As her anxiety escalated, the baby within her kicked forcefully against her abdomen. Stella was calling Ian's name... and he was commanding her to scream louder. *How had he gotten her wet?* Naa Akweley wondered. Had he flicked her nipples with his rough tongue? Had he suckled on them until Stella shuddered in delight? Was he getting harder with each vigorous thrust? Could Stella manage to keep her stubby legs wrapped around his sinewy waist? For some reason, Naa Akweley thought about the silk bedspread she had spent hours hunting for just a month ago. She hoped they wouldn't ruin it.

Ian had an insatiable need to make love, but he had hardly touched Naa Akweley since she began showing. She ached so much for him. She wanted desperately to go upstairs and stop the errant pair in their tracks... to beat Ian over his head and ask him what the hell he thought he was doing!

But she couldn't.

In a trance, her feet carried her to Ian's study instead.

A good wife never complains. A good wife keeps her husband happy. A good wife…

Naa Akweley paused her mantra long enough to pour herself a glass of scotch. As the hot liquid coursed down her constricted throat, her baby slowly stopped kicking and she began to sob violently. She kept her fist over her mouth so that the sound of her pain did not rise above Ian's moans of wicked, unholy pleasure.

Not again, God. Not again.

****

Afosua sat in her car and waited for the jitters she was feeling to wear off. The encounter with Naa Akweley had not gone anywhere near as planned. She had been ready for Naa Akweley to object to travel for several reasons: a church conference… a dress fitting… or whatever it was that first ladies of churches did with their spare time. But Naa Akweley was right in one regard – Afosua had not considered that she wouldn't be able to travel because of her pregnancy. Afosua could have overcome this objection rationally if Naa Akweley hadn't thrown her private life into her face like a filthy handkerchief. Afosua had always prided herself about being calm under pressure and generally very pragmatic, but something about Naa Akweley's demeanor always rattled her. She might not ever discover what about the woman offended her most, since had essentially told the formidable Mrs. Blankson to go to hell that afternoon.

Afosua tried to turn her thoughts towards problems she could actually solve. But she could not ignore that she had lost a useful ally in Naa Akweley – or in her husband, rather.

Ian Blankson was the senior pastor in one of Ghana's three mega-churches, and his congregation included statesmen, business leaders and all manner of scoundrels willing to pay a pretty pesewa for their salvation. More importantly, the wives and mistresses of these men thronged to Ian's church in hoards: they were Afosua's true target. She was going to get to them by aligning herself intimately with Naa Akweley. Or she would have had she not responded so appallingly to the woman's taunts.

Afosua buried herself in her work for the rest of the day, trying to sort out the details of two accounts that were left on her desk. She quickly analyzed the risks involved in the Bawku venture. The skirmishes that plagued the small Northern town were no longer a threat, and the eccentric Ashanti investor who wanted to set up a beef processing plant would do well there. The people were eager to see new investment and natural resources were plentiful. However, it would be up to the investor to generate enough bribe money to satisfy the MP for the region. The behavior analysis of the MP showed him to be highly deceptive and greedy but amenable to permit significant change for his region, especially with the right amount of compensation and recognition.

She moved on to the next account: the Swedes.

By 7 pm it was dark outside and she was still pouring over the details of this account. Something just didn't add up. It was *too* perfect. There was absolutely no risk. To the untrained mind, the project seemed like a no-brainer, and a

Godsend... but Afosua knew better. Nothing is ever certain. Everything has a price.

"What do you have there?"

The sound of Mr. Boakye's voice jolted Afosua from her intense thoughts.

"The Swedish account," she replied brightly. "I'm looking over the behavior analysis grid and the numbers. Something's not quite right."

Mr. Boakye's face darkened.

"That's not your account," he said tersely.

"Yeah, I know. And that's actually something I wanted to talk to you and Mr. Phillips about. When you contracted me, you promised me a spot in upper management. Ever since I got here, I've had the title – yes – but not the responsibility. All you've had me do is the work of a first year analyst and I..."

Harold Boakye held up his hand, cutting her off and signaling for silence.

"You know what your problem is, Ms. Gyemfi?" He seated himself on the edge of her desk. "You haven't been vetted yet. You are neither tested nor proven. Everyone – *anyone* - who has ever advanced within this company possesses one thing that sets them apart and makes them special."

"You mean a penis?" Afosua retorted, her tone acerbic.

Harold Boakye chuckled dryly.

"Experience. Everyone here has real world, applicable experience. You, my dear, have none."

"I will as soon as I hash out this Swedish account," she replied confidently. "Sir," she added.

"No. No you won't. That account is too important and too detailed, even for you," said Mr. Boakye. "Brilliant as you may be, you are not to touch it."

"But –."

"Do NOT touch that account, Ms. Gyemfi," Mr. Boakye said, rising from his perch and taking the file with him. "That is all."

Afosua nodded obediently and bid him a good night before preparing to leave herself. Too bad for Mr. Boakye she had already saved on the data on her pen drive. She waited to hear the click of his keys locking his office door before dropping it into her purse.

*****

Naa Akweley was still in the study when Ian walked in. The smell of liquor and the spirit of her despair clouded the room. She looked up and greeted her husband with red-rimmed, watery eyes. He looked back with disgust.

"You're drunk," he spat.

"Yes I am."

"How dare you drink, in your condition?"

"How dare you fuck the maid, in my condition!" she shot back.

When he slapped her, she momentarily lost her vision. When she regained it, all she could see was the hulking frame of her husband looming over her. She hated him... hated and still loved him so much.

"You know that we have dinner with the Bishop tonight," he railed. "You know how important this meeting is, especially at this time!"

Naa Akweley nodded in hasty agreement. She cast her eyes downward, showing her remorse.

"Ian, I'm sorry...I am. I was just so upset because when I came home you... you were –"

She couldn't even bring herself to say it. She didn't have to.

"What I do in my own house, with my own staff, is my business. Your only JOB as my wife is to keep me happy. You don't have to concern yourself with anything else," he said menacingly. "Understood?"

Naa Akweley swallowed hard. She completely understood why her husband was sleeping with the maid. Who would ever believe it? He was a 'man of God' and Stella was an illiterate nobody from nowhere. Any allegations she might ever make would be laughed out of court or the newspapers. Some would believe her, but most would not. And so what if he was? He could always blame his folly on the influence of the devil.

Ian's voice cut into her and ended her silent reflection. He had been talking, but she was barely paying attention.

"You've never had to work a day in your life," he finished. "Don't start acting up or it won't always be that way. Get yourself cleaned up. We leave in 45 minutes."

When Ian left the room, Naa Akweley allowed herself a few more minutes of self-pity and wept, before gathering the strength to go up to her and her husband's bedroom. At least the maid had had the decency to make the bed. Of course, she would have to be sacked. This was the third maid. Naa Akweley would not stand for a third miscarriage brought on by grief. If nothing else, she was strong enough to do that. She was strong enough to save this baby.

The drive from Labone to Tema was long and stressful. Annette hating driving, but if she wanted any sort of independence it was a skill she had to develop. When she had gotten married, her husband insisted on a driver taking her everywhere she wanted to go. She had loathed the idea. A driver limited her freedoms and one slip of his loose lips could have ruined her life. Over the course of time, she persuaded Alex, the newest chauffer Mr. Prah had hired, to teach her how to drive. In exchange, Alex would get the majority of the lesson days off and keep his pay. All he had to do was pick her up in the morning and then park the car in the garage at night, no questions asked. Alex readily agreed. Annette was surprised at how easy it was to convince him. She wondered if it was because Alex was abysmally lazy or completely mesmerized by her breasts as she thrust them in his face as she made her proposal. She honestly felt bad for manipulating him.

When Annette got to Community 11, she parked her car, sat outside of Sophia Ike's house and slipped off her wedding ring. She shoved it into her pocket and rang the gate bell.

The watchman opened it up and let her in.

"Good evening, Idrisu," she said quietly.

"Good evening madam!" he replied cheerily.

Idrisu liked Annette very much. She was one of the few people who greeted him like a man and not a servant. He always took good care to look after her car when she came to see Sophia.

"Please, madam is inside," he informed her pleasantly, ushering her towards the door.

"Thank you, Idrisu," she smiled.

Idrisu felt his pants stiffen as he watched Annette walk away. Her firm buttocks swayed seductively but innocently with every step she took. And her hair – how he loved her hair! It was thick and curly and always carried a fresh scent that reminded him of the dawn. If only he were richer, more educated and younger... maybe then they could wake up and watch the coming of dawn everyday together.

He rubbed his throbbing penis and went back to his guard post, pleasuring himself with his forbidden fantasy of Ms. Annette.

When Annette walked into the house, Sophia was in the kitchen.

"Hello dear!" Annette called.

Sophia smiled and kissed Annette on the cheek.

"I'm so glad you were able to make it by before you went home."

"Yeah, it was a pretty tough afternoon," Annette sighed, rubbing her neck. "Naa Akweley and Afosua got into it today. I thought it might come to blows in the end. Thankfully, it didn't."

"Oh?" Sophia pressed. "What happened?"

She passed Annette a small bottle of chilled water. Annette gratefully accepted it.

"Apparently Afosua has some sort of project up her sleeve," Annette began. "She wants to take Naa Akweley and I up to Dumbai for a girls' weekend. She said it is a place every woman should go to at least once."

Sophia nodded.

"I'm familiar with Dumbai. My dad went there once when he was a government surveyor... before all the Nigerians were sacked from Ghana in the 70s," she said wryly. "He said it was lovely."

"Really? I'd love for you to join us if we do go!"

"Do you think your friends will be okay with that?" Sophia asked cautiously. "You know I'm not a part of their 'group.'"

Annette giggled. She loved the way Sophia spoke. Her Nigerian accent made her sincere concern sound aggressive, almost angry. It resonated with Annette. She wished she could be more like Sophia.

"It doesn't matter. I don't think we're going anyway. Naa called Afosua some choice names, Afosua shot back, and I just sat there like a bump on a log watching the whole thing unfold. What could I do? You know how superior Naa Akweley is."

Sophia handed her a bowl of pepper soup, which Annette accepted with her left hand. This made Sophia snatch it back.

"Sorry I used my left!" Annette apologized. "I know it's rude."

"No," Sophia said, shaking her head, "it's not that. You're not wearing your wedding ring."

"Yes... and?"

"We both know you're married, so why pretend you're not?"

"Because I don't want any more reminders of my husband - of my LIFE – than necessary," Annette snapped.

"Okay, okay! I'm sorry," Sophia said quickly. "Here's your soup."

Annette spooned her soup into her mouth slowly, her thoughts now on the husband whom she had tried all day to forget. Every morning she made it a point to mentally eliminate his existence until she was forced to face him at home. He was an old man – over 70. He was also fabulously wealthy but there was nothing he could provide for her that was of value. He was not her friend and he was too old to be her lover. When he touched her she was immediately repulsed. There were many nights that she lay in her bed, still as a corpse, until he had finished using her unresponsive body to pleasure himself. When he was done, he would retreat to his bedroom, crawling away like a slug to its muddy hole. She was grateful that she at least did not have to share a room with him.

Annette's marriage to Kwame Prah was the result of a joke. Sadly, no one was laughing after it was over – no one but Mr. Prah. Annette's father was a Lebanese merchant who had fallen on hard times many years ago, and Mr. Prah was a shipping tycoon and one of the few African men to break into an industry that was traditionally dominated by Europeans, Arabs and now, the Chinese. As an outsider, he had to be more cutthroat than his rivals. It was the only way his business had survived the four decades of *coup d'etats*, food shortages and other upheavals that ravaged West Africa. Through it all, Mr. Prah remained untouched by calamity. His shrewd business acumen and ruthlessness had only served him in amassing more and more wealth over the years.

Annette despised him. The stink of fetid ocean water and industrial waste clung to his leathery skin. The old toad always had a smug smiled that played around his lips, but only truly broke out when it was apparent that others around him were suffering. A sudden flash of his crooked, yellow teeth made Annette shudder.

Abdul Fawaz had sought out a loan from Mr. Prah when his daughter was six years old. The 'joke' between the two men was that if Annette's father was unable to repay the borrowed amount in seven years, then he would give Annette away in marriage to Kwame Prah. A week after Annette turned thirteen, Kwame Prah showed up at Abdul's doorstep to whisk her away, much to the shock of the entire household.

"A deal is a deal," he grinned sinisterly, gripping Annette's little hand in his.

That was almost 30 years ago, in the 80s when the famine had struck and things were going badly for everyone. Things had gotten a little better for Annette's family, but not quickly enough to pay the enormous debt. Abdul begged for Annette's forgiveness and promised to pay the debt if she would just go with Mr. Prah for a little while. He just needed a little more time. What could she do, seeing her father so broken? But to their shock, Mr. Prah would not agree to any extensions on the loan. It was all or Annette. She left with Mr. Prah the next morning. In an odd act of kindness, he let her finish school and married her on her 18th birthday. She had never seen the world, outside of the confines of Mr. Prah's permission. By herself she was a nobody.

Sophia watched Annette struggle with her thoughts and reached over to wipe away her tears of distress.

"I know what you're thinking, and it's going to be okay... I promise."

Annette sniffed and nodded. She gave Sophia a brave smile.

"Come with me," Sophia said softly, holding her hand. She led Annette into the guest bedroom and shut the door.

"It's going to be okay," she whispered as she slowly began to kiss Annette, pulling expertly at the knot on her wrap dress. Annette was instantly disrobed, her dress falling to the floor in a soft heap.

Sophia made quick work of her bra, never stopping the torrent of soft wet kisses that she delivered to Annette's anticipating lips. Annette moaned with pleasure, closing her eyes and welcoming Sophia's skilled seduction. Sophia pushed Annette to the edge of the bed, lifting each of her legs and removing her white lace panties. When Annette was completely naked, Sophia threw off the bright orange and green boubou she was wearing for the evening. There was nothing underneath. She had been waiting for Annette all day.

Placing her hand between Annette's thighs, she traced her tongue down the younger woman's neck, stopping at her belly button and teasing her with flicks of her tongue, running her lips over the expanse of her small, taut belly, biting her softly when she saw fit. Annette shuddered in anticipation.

"Sophia... please..."

Sophia smiled and spread Annette open, hungrily devouring the wetness that was waiting for her. She tasted so sweet, so sloppy, like a ripe mango on a dry Harmattan afternoon, and Sophia was thirsty. She felt like a youth stealing from her neighbor's backyard, and the audacity of it excited her. When she had had her fill, she sucked Annette's clitoris gently at first, and finally with more urgency. Sophia moaned, too, knowing how much pleasure Annette was receiving. When Annette could take it no longer, she collapsed backward on the bed, clutching Sophia by the head, her most intimate and secret places screaming silently as she climaxed. Finally, she allowed a gurgle of delight to pass over her lips as she stared at the swirling ceiling fan above, riveted by the rhythmic rising and falling of her chest.

"I love you, Sophia," she whispered in the darkness.

"I know."

They lay entangled in one another, blending the smells of lilac and violet from the perfumes misting from their warm skin. The scent of sex clung to the cool cotton sheets.

Idrisu stood under the starry night sky looking up at the broken bathroom window from where the sounds of the two women's lovemaking always escaped. Heart pounding and palms wet, he wiped his hand on his handkerchief and went back to his guard station.

This was always his favorite part.

Two weeks had passed since Afosua had seen Tony. She was surprised at how frequently her thoughts had turned to him in the days since she had unceremoniously dropped him off at a street corner and driven off. Unaccustomed to this new sensation, she decided to seek him out.

It would be easy enough to find Tony. All she had to do was show up at New Spirit International Church which, although a house of worship, was now hostile territory for her. Still, she had to investigate and resolve her new infatuation.

"I'll be taking a long lunch today," Afosua informed Gertrude. "If anyone is looking for me, they can always reach me on my BB."

"I'll let them know." Gertrude spoke absently. She was pouring over a stack of reports that one of the analysts had dropped on her desk.

Afosua had become more and more impressed with Gertrude. She was taking a real interest in the company and looking for ways to involve herself in work outside of her receptionist duties. Afosua recognized this, and hoped that the other managers had as well - or at least or soon would.

The drive through town was uncommonly smooth. New Spirit was located in Dzorwulu and Afosua had prepared herself to face the beast known as Traffic, the long grinding, jerking metal serpent that typically crawls its way through Accra's blacktop roads. But perhaps luck was on her side. Perhaps the smooth ride was a metaphor for good things to come? She'd soon find out.

She pulled her car into a vacant spot near the front of the door of the mega-church. The high stone archway seemed imposing and not very welcoming. The gardens that surrounded the exterior were well manicured and pleasing to the eye, but the whole aura seemed very forced and artificial.

A lot like Naa Akweley, Afosua thought as she swung the heavy glass doors open.

A pretty receptionist greeted Afosua as she walked in. Her static blond shoulder length weave barely moved as she spoke.

"Welcome to New Spirit International Church," she slurred with a fake American accent. "How ken I hulp yew?"

Afosua was bewildered by the girl's Locally Acquired Foreign Accent and pressed her lips into a smirk to keep from laughing outright. She couldn't begrudge the child for wanting to appear exotic. After all, she lived in a country where almost everyone looked and sounded the same. Still, she looked and sounded ridiculous.

"Good afternoon," Afosua returned. "I'm looking for the church accountant, Mr. Tony…"

Afosua froze, realizing she didn't even know his last name. She was surprised that she hadn't taken the time to research him better. What was going on with her?

"Tony Coffie?"

Afosua swung around and almost bumped into Ian Blankson, senior pastor of the church. His broad shoulders strained against the seams of his dark suit, as if begging to expose the brawny body beneath it. Ian's eyes were boring into hers. She was startled to discover flecks of green in his irises and suddenly realized he was standing much too close. She raised an eyebrow and composed herself.

"Yes," she smiled with mock appreciation. "Mr. Coffie."

Ian Blankson's eyes roved all over her body. She couldn't determine if he wanted to eat her or toy with her. Whatever his intentions, Afosua recognized a predator when she met one. She squared her shoulders so that she stood taller and more confident.

"He doesn't work here," Ian informed her.

"Oh. I see."

Afosua's heart sank. Their brief tryst had cost Tony his job, and she was truly sorry for it.

"Mr. Coffie has his own accountancy practice," Ian continued. "He contracts with the church. We don't employ him directly."

"Oh... I see."

"Come into my office and I'll give you all his details," Ian purred invitingly.

Afosua didn't know much about Ian Blankson, but she had the feeling that she didn't want to be alone behind closed doors with him.

"I'm sure your receptionist can give me all the information I need," she said firmly. "That is her job after all, is it not?"

Ian chuckled.

"It is indeed. Mary, please give the lady whatever she needs."

He turned on the ball of his foot and padded into the sanctuary like a beast in search of its next victim. Afosua caught Mary's eye as she stared adoringly at the retreating back of her pastor... or possible paramour.

"The number if you will, Mary."

"Yels. Herrrr yew are mademe," the young lady yawned.

Afosua wished her a good day and left. If nothing else, she had succeeded in getting a good laugh at Mary's expense. But she had discovered something even more valuable: Ian Blankson was not a man to be trusted, no matter what his credentials read. This man was not genuine. Her intuition was never wrong.

*****

It was 2 o'clock and Annette had let time get away from her. She scurried to the driver's side of her car and sped off, racing against time and traffic. She was supposed to be accompanying her husband to a luncheon with his colleagues at 2:30. Mr. Prah was finally retiring and his company was feting him with a farewell party. The man should have retired ages ago, but he was such a control freak that he could not let go of the reins of power. She picked Alex up from the chop bar where he hung out and ordered him to race to the house.

Annette was still tingling from where Sophia had spent the late morning playing with her. What was supposed to be an innocent few hours looking over designs for a new dress turned into a passionate marathon with Annette straddled across Sophia's lap and Sophia's fingers stroking stroked her clitoris until she climaxed again and again. The thought of it excited Annette even more. As she bolted into her home, she hoped the smell of recent sex did not betray her.

"You're late," scolded Mr. Prah coldly.

"Darling! I'm so sorry. I was delayed..."

Mr. Prah cut her off.

"Go upstairs and get dressed at once. Your hair looks a mess. Fix that too."

The moment the words left his mouth, a sudden thought occurred to him. That wicked tramp..

"Wait, Annette," said Mr. Prah, striding purposefully towards her. He grabbed her by the wrist and whipped her around.

"I may be old, but I'm not stupid. Whoever this other man is, end it now. I will not share you with another man, and I damn well will not care for his bastard! I'll see you in the street before I do!"

Annette lifted her chin and looked him squarely in the eye. Her tone was sincere and deliberate.

"Darling, I promise you: There IS no other man. There is no man in my life but you."

He searched for the truth in her fair brown eyes. When he saw no deceit, he relaxed the grip on her arm.

"Go get dressed," he said softly. "I'm sorry I was so hard with you."

"Forgive me," she said, kissing his gnarled hand. "It was my fault for being late. Let me rush quickly so that we won't be so late, okay?"

He sent her on her way patting her soft buttocks and watching it jiggle wantonly as she retreated down the long hallway to her room. His erection was snuffed as quickly as it had sprung. Going after her to the bedroom would only frustrate him more. Mr. Prah called the driver around and waited for his wife to join him in the back seat of his new BMW, where he could fondle her to his heart's content. His colleagues would recognize the sweet scent of the flesh between her legs on his hands and they'd all be jealous. He chuckled gleefully at the thought and nestled his head on the grey leather headrest.

****

Afosua couldn't help but feel disappointed that her search for Tony had been fruitless. She couldn't shake the hint of shame that she had actually gone on the prowl for him. She was accustomed to men coming to her, and to picking or dismissing them as she saw fit. The memory of Tony had yet to release its grip on her subconscious. It was a maddening, insatiable itch that she had no way of scratching.

She didn't go back to the office directly. Instead she drove aimlessly around the city, trying to clear her mind. By the time she did get back, her colleagues were preparing to leave. She decided she would work late in order to divert her thoughts.

When she opened the door, she was pleasantly surprised to see Gertrude still at her desk. Gertrude was intently staring at her screen and hardly noticed Afosua walk in. Afosua smiled at the younger woman, pleased with idea that she was so dedicated to her fledgling career. If she kept this up, she would be unstoppable.

"Hi, what are you doing working on this late?" Afosua asked, peering over the top of Gertrude's screen.

Gertrude whipped around.

"I was just finishing some reports!" she yelled a little too loudly, clicking frantically on her mouse.

Afosua smiled. The girl was quick, but not quick enough to minimize the bold blue and white social networking site she was trawling. Perhaps she wouldn't go as far as Afosua had imagined. She stepped around Gertrude's desk and thumbed through a stack of magazines on the cane coffee table that sat in the waiting room.

"Any messages for me?" Afosua asked out of habit. "I was gone longer than I expected."

"No... er... that is yes. You had a visitor. A Mr. Coffie came to see you," stumbled Gertrude.

"Tony? Tony Coffie?"

"Yes."

Afosua was exasperated.

"Well why didn't you BBM me?" she practically wailed.

"Well... he said he didn't want to leave a message. He said he would much rather..."

"...wait for you in your office," finished a rich male voice.

Tony leaned against the frame of Afosua's office door, looking sheepish.

"I hope I didn't get your assistant into too much trouble," he apologized. "Wherever you had gone, I didn't want you rushing back on my account – so I decided to wait. I didn't mind waiting."

Afosua sighed in relief. There was no reason Tony had to know she had gone searching for him. She could still maintain an air of superiority, if she really wanted to. But playing mind tricks with him was not on her immediate agenda. In that moment all she could think of was how handsome Tony looked in his dark grey slacks and azure shirt. He smelled divine and he looked different – better - than she recalled.

"No, no! It's no trouble at all. I just don't like not being in the know when it comes to clients and visitors, that's all."

Gertrude *hmmm*'d under her breath and began to pack up her things. She slung her purse over her shoulder and slipped her heels onto her feet. Gertrude always took her shoes off at her desk, which drove Afosua mad.

"I'm going to leave now Ms. Gyemfi, if that's okay."

"Absolutely. See you in the morning."

"Good night, Gertrude," whispered Tony. "Thank you for keeping me entertained."

Gertrude flashed him a broad, girlish smile and left the room. Afosua was bewildered. Just how exactly had Gertrude 'entertained' Tony? Given the woman's history with Robert and broom closets, Afosua could only imagine. Surprised by her sudden feelings of anger, she brushed by Tony as she stomped into her office.

"Shut the door please," she commanded. She was miffed at the thought of Tony flirting with Gertrude and wasn't sure how happy she was to see him anymore. She turned and faced him with her arms across her chest.

"How did you find me?"

"I did some asking around," Tony replied mischievously. "Honestly I just picked up one of your business cards from your desk before I left your house; it made the finding much easier."

"So you're a pick pocket," she snapped. "And what brings you to see me?"

"I couldn't get you off my mind," he admitted, moving in closer. "I came here to – to –"

"To what?!?"

She was annoyed and sucked her teeth in frustration.

Tony grabbed Afosua suddenly and kissed her deeply. As his lips roamed hers insistently she felt her defenses weaken. He gently moved her arms from their position of defense and placed them around his neck, willing her to welcome him. As she melted against him, she felt him get harder and harder. This had to be a dream. How was he here in her office, just when she'd needed him? She didn't care. She closed her eyes and groaned with anticipation, wondering what might come next.

"Burning the candle at both ends are we?" said an amused voice from the shadows.

It was Robert. He was standing at the door with a glass of water in his hand, grinning devilishly. Tony and Afosua broke away from each other, startled by the interruption. Afosua cursed under her breath before turning towards her colleague who was obviously having a lot of fun at her expense.

 "Can I help you, Robert?" She spoke tersely.

"No! I was just about to lock up and I saw your light on. Wouldn't want you to be trapped in here alone, that's all." He paused and cackled wickedly before he spoke again. "But then, I guess there's no chance of that, is there?"

"You're right," Afosua replied. "We were just leaving."

She picked up her suit jacket and walked briskly towards the door. Tony followed close behind her, licking the taste of her flavored gloss from his lips. He nodded goodbye to Robert, who offered the pair a piece of congenial advice.

"Next time if you need a little privacy, try the broom closet!"

"No thank you! There have been too many rodents frequenting it lately," Afosua tossed in retort.

Robert was too self-absorbed to ever make idle gossip about discovering Tony and Afosua. Besides, it would be to his disadvantage, given that his own reputation was not unsoiled. It would come off as petty. Afosua wasn't concerned about his loose lips – unlike Tony's, which she was very interested in.

 "Let's go to my place," she suggested. "We won't have any interruptions there."

*****

Naa Akweley sat at her dressing table, hardly able to look at her own reflection in the mirror. How had she become this woman? Ian was touching her all the time now, but only with his fist. Tonight he had blackened her eye because she served rice for dinner instead of potatoes. She rationalized that he must be under a lot of stress with the church, that's must be why he was so angry all the time. The council of archbishops was considering elevating him from a senior pastor to bishop, and everything had to be perfect. Naa knew that she had to make major changes if she wanted to have a happy home. Everything had to be flawless.

But the pain from the beatings was more than skin deep. This, and the isolation, was driving a knife into her soul. She was dying. She could feel it.

Who could she talk to? Her own family had distanced themselves from her after she married Ian, and she knew she was utterly alone. Somehow she had managed to alienate the majority of her friends, too. Her personality had become so poisonous that she wondered if it was even accurate to classify them as friends. She didn't even like being alone with herself. Perhaps... perhaps if she tried apologizing?

She ached to talk to someone – anyone! Naa Akweley picked up her cell phone and searched for the number of the one person who might understand what it was like to be a hollow woman searching to be made whole. She let it ring once before hanging up and weeping in despair.

A good wife never embarrasses her husband.

*****

43

Afosua watched Tony pull his navy blue Nissan next to her car as they parked in her courtyard. He got out quickly and scampered over to her door to help her out of the vehicle. She was genuinely surprised and a little embarrassed. She wasn't used to men waiting on her in any capacity. She'd never felt that she needed them to.

"At least this time, I can drive myself home," he joked. "No more dropping me off at corners!"

Afosua let her guard down enough to laugh with him. The sun had just set and the sky was awash with the colors of pink, amber and blood red. No matter how many times she saw it, she was always amazed by the beauty of a sunset in Accra. This was just one of the many simple reasons she was glad she made the decision to move back home. A hoarse voice called for her from the veranda, disturbing her reverie. At times it was this voice that that made her not so glad to be back.

"Afos! Is that you?"

"Yes, Ma," she sighed.

"Come into the house. I haven't seen you in three days," her mother complained.

Afosua took Tony up to the veranda where her mother was seated, having her signature cocktail of Club beer and Sprite. At 58, Elizabeth Anaan was still an attractive woman, with a figure rivaling girls in their 20s. Her good looks were the result of being a kept woman... a very well kept woman. Elizabeth was Afosua's father's mistress until the day he died.

"Who is this?" Elizabeth asked suspiciously.

"Tony Coffie," Tony answered, offering his hand to shake that of the elder woman. "And judging by your impeccable stature, I assume that you are the mother of Ms. Gyemfi?"

"A flatterer! Huh. Let me tell you something young man, in this house, flattery will get you anywhere you like. Have a seat!"

She was smiling. Tony was relieved. Afosua was aghast. She just wanted to get the man to her wing of the house so he could unlock the mystery of why he was so unforgettable! Now he was having a drink with her mother instead. She turned her lips downward to keep from sucking her teeth in frustration.

For the next two hours, Tony regaled Madam Anaan with tales of his travels and his work. The more scandalous the story, the more hooked she was. She loved to hear about other people's financial woes and triumphs. To his credit Tony refused to divulge the names of any of his clients no matter how hard she pressed. By the time the two had finished, Madam Anaan was drunk, sleepy and thoroughly impressed with the young man.

"You have to come back and visit me sometime," she commanded. "Ever since Afos' dad died, I've been quite lonely in the house."

Tony shot Afosua a confused look. She turned her face away from his.

"I thought...?" he stopped himself from going further. He smiled and looked at Elizabeth kindly. "Yes, of course I will come and visit you."

Afosua's mother got up and excused herself. She was going to retire for the evening and indulge in the latest Nigerian film that the houseboy had procured for her. It was likely that she would pass out in front of the TV.

"Good night, Tony. It was a pleasure meeting you."

"Good night, Madam."

Afosua smiled wearily and wished her mother goodnight before sauntering toward her living quarters. Her father had built her wing adjacent to the main house when she moved to England to study.

"That way, when you come back home you will have your own place to stay, but never be too far from me," he said lovingly. He knew how much she valued her independence and he indulged her whenever he could. Afosua's pleasant memories of her father softened her tone towards Tony.

"Would you like to come up? I'd offer you a drink, but it looks like you and my mother had plenty between the two of you."

She laughed nervously when he didn't respond. He was looking at her intently. She hadn't seen that look in a man's eye in a long time. Finally, Tony grasped her slender hands and pulled her close to him, whispering in her ear.

"Afosua – I have something to confess to you. I don't know what it is about you, but I want you to know that I don't just want to make love to you, I want to make you love me."

This made Afosua freeze. When Tony looked in her eyes, he saw a sadness overshadow them. It was almost as if she was mourning.

"That can never happen Tony," Afosua answered coldly. "I could never love anyone. And if that is your sole intention, I think it's best that you go on home."

"But..."

"Good night, Tony. You know your way back to the main road, don't you? The watchman will let you out."

She walked into her front door and shut it without looking back. Tony stood stunned in the courtyard for a few moments before driving off. When she heard the heavy metal gate swing shut, Afosua dropped her limp body onto her sofa and stared blankly at the ceiling, refusing to agonize over another lost opportunity for love. She would not cry. What for? Crying never solved anything.

Annette rested her chin in the palm of her right hand and sighed. Keeping her expression neutral was proving difficult. She focused her gaze on the dazzling colors dancing on the crystal goblets on the dining table. She looked above and saw its source: an enormous, gilded chandelier flickering gaily, secured by a cable draped in golden silk. She should have been impressed but, despite the general splendor, her feelings were grim.

Mr. Prah was giggling foolishly with old school mates and businessmen who he had been making deals with for almost half a century. Unlike him, many of these men had retired from work many years before. They had come to understand, perhaps grudgingly, that they did not have the skills to compete in the new age of technology and social networking. However, one of the old leeches had managed to procure a handheld gadget and was showing the rest of them something that had them all guffawing like they were back in a dingy dorm room. It struck Annette that this group of men was content to enter a new phase of life and indulge in frivolous pursuits, unlike her husband who had resisted relinquishing the reins of power. Until now. She wasn't sure what had motivated him to suddenly retire, particularly since he made it a point to never discuss his business dealings with her.

Mr. Prah shrouded himself in gloomy mystery.

There was one of his puzzles Annette was immediately able to crack though. Her boredom turned to dismay when she saw Mr. Prah pass his left hand under the nostrils of one of his old chums – the same hand he had used to finger her with just an hour before. As both men doubled over in laughter, she fought hard against the waves of shame washing over her.

Annette turned her attention back to the crystal place settings on the dinner table. There was no one she could really talk to in this circle. In the past, when she had tried to engage other couples who attended company dinners, the women would have nothing to do with her and the men dared not. There was a rumor that she was a gold-digger and that consorting with Mr. Prah's younger and very attractive wife, even casually, would only get you sacked. It was considered too costly to show her kindness or courtesy. She was left alone, therefore, and felt very alone. Annette drank her wine sullenly and thought of Sophia.

The lace and silk gown she was wearing was Sophia's creation. Sophia Ike was an established couturier, renowned for her skill at mixing Nigerian and Western materials to create exciting garments. She had a small but very influential clientele, and was so sought after that she could pick and choose who wore her exclusive designs. There was no mistaking a Sophia Ike piece.

"My clothing isn't for everyone," Sophia once bragged during an interview. "My garments are not for the masses. There is only an exclusive group women confident enough to carry my designs."

And it was true. The women who wore an Ike original were picked for the clothes, not the other way around. Affluent men regularly traipsed into Sophia's design house in search of a one of a kind creation for their women. To own an Ike original was a badge of distinction. Sophia fed this frenzy by daring to turn away any number of potential high profile clients a few times a year. It was a mad strategy that turned out to be nothing short of brilliant. Annette had once accused her of stealing a page from the American embassy's visa policy of wantonly 'bouncing' clients just for the sheer shock of it.

She wistfully buried herself in the memory of the day they had met.

After several unsuccessful attempts to get his wife seen for a fitting with Sophia three years ago, Kwame Prah had eventually given up, telling Annette it was impossible. When she voiced her disappointment, he dismissively told her that she was welcome to try if she felt she could do better. He was done.

Annette couldn't accept it. She burst into Sophia Ike's studio, demanding a fitting. It was uncharacteristic of her to make a scene, but she felt entitled to something good and special in her life, given all she had suffered.

"I want to see Ms. Ike," Annette said loudly to the designer's assistant that fateful Thursday afternoon.

"I'm afraid you can't without an appointment, and I'm going to have to ask you to leave if you don't have one," replied the impeccably dressed woman. Her bright red lips were turned downward in a sneer.

Annette continued yelling her demands until the commotion brought Sophia from her back office. She looked Annette over slowly and carefully before speaking.

"What's all this noise?" she demanded in her thick accent.

Upon seeing the icon, Annette froze. The boldness she had previously summoned abandoned her quickly. Annette was struck by how beautiful Sophia was and how, despite her reputation for being a bitch, something in her air appeared very kind. Sophia also instantly assessed Annette. Seeing past the display of bravado, she saw a woman who was elegant and demure but did not know her self-worth. She saw in Annette a woman who had never been loved, at least not properly.

"And what is your name, madam?" Sophia inquired, her tone frosty.

"Annette. Annette Prah," she stammered. "I – I'm sorry to bust in like this..."

Sophia cut her off and turned to her assistant.

"Esi, don't take any more appointments for the next two hours. I'm going to fit Ms. Prah."

The slender aide was taken aback. Sophia never saw anyone uninvited, particularly not someone who displayed such rudeness. Annette on the other hand was overjoyed. She had taken a chance and by pure luck it had worked! She reached out to shake Sophia Ike's hand.

"Oh thank you!" she gushed excitedly.

As she took Sophia's hand in hers she felt something course through every fiber of her body. It felt as if there was a volt of power surging between the two women. Annette didn't know which made her more uncomfortable: her racing heart or her now arid mouth. She wondered if Sophia felt it too or if it was just her imagination. Unable to speak further, Annette dutifully followed Sophia, who was beckoning her into a fitting room.

The private fitting room was decorated to give the feel of an 18th century French boudoir. The walls were dusty rose with a silvery white trim, and sported art from every corner of Africa. There were twelve female mannequins clothed in Sophia's coveted apparel, each very different from the next. They were posed in a circle as if engaged in conversation. Each mannequin seemed to be judging the other.

Just like real women do, Annette thought.

Among all this finery were little objects made of seashells and butter tins – the type that poor children crafted and sold in busy streets. Sophia Ike was proving to be a confusing character, indeed.

"You'll have to take off your clothes," Sophia said without looking at Annette.

She picked up a measuring tape and some chalk from the other end of the room. When Annette was disrobed, Sophia finally turned to face her. Her long colorful robe skimmed the floor, making each step appear as though she were gliding. She slid her hands between Annette's toned thighs and over the expanse of her curvy hips. She scribbled numbers on a small black slate.

"My fittings are very intimate, which is why I don't do them with everyone," she explained. "Any tailor can throw together some material based on inches and centimeters, but MY clothes are living, breathing garments. Just like the wearer, they have a story. I want to make sure that the stories of the wearer and my clothes are compatible. Do you understand?"

Annette nodded dutifully. She tried to keep her focus on professional thoughts and willed her knees not to buckle. She had asked for this, after all.

Sophia stopped her exploration of Annette's curves and looked deeply into her almond colored eyes.

"I need to see your nipples."

"Excuse me...what?"

"Take off your bra. How else will I know if this material matches your skin?"

Annette did as she was told. Clad only in her black thong, she felt oddly secure. As harsh as Sophia was, she felt safe in her presence. She drew a deep breath when Sophia stood behind her and cupped her breasts, thumbing her now taunt nipples rhythmically. She swallowed deeply before she spoke next.

"Is this part of this fitting process?" Annette asked, unsure that she should be questioning Sophia at all.

"No," Sophia admitted. "This I am doing for my own pleasure... and for yours."

The pair were facing the three paneled mirror that covered the broadest wall of the fitting room. Amazed, Annette watched Sophia's soft brown hand plunge into her waistband of her panties and steadied herself as her fingers merged with the wetness of her clitoris. Sophia was nibbling on her back, causing the blood to rush to the surface of her caramel colored skin. Sophia stopped to make eye contact with Annette who was looking at their joint reflection in the mirror and losing herself in the first orgasm she'd ever had in her life.

"A penny for your thoughts?" said an inquisitive male voice.

"Eh? Oh... Victor. Hi! How are you?"

Mr. Prah's son was speaking to her, jerking her away from her pleasurable recollections. Annette didn't mind though. Although Victor bore a striking resemblance to his father, he was not quite as piggish and was unquestionably kinder. He was Kwame Prah's youngest son and, at age 40, one of Annette's three stepchildren. Incidentally, he had also been her senior at the boarding school Mr. Prah had sent her to.

Victor had never made a secret about his feelings for Annette and wondered why she never returned his affections. When his father had come to visit him at school, always insisting on bringing something for Annette, he thought the old man was just being kind to the impressionable student. He never could have imagined that his aged father would marry the woman he had hoped to ask to do the same one day.

"I'm well," said Victor, settling in next to her at the dinner table. "The old man seems to be really enjoying himself."

"Yes. Yes he does look happy."

Annette was relieved to have a break in her thoughts. Victor was one of the few people who didn't care about the idle gossip that swirled around her, and he made it a point to show her modest affection whenever he saw her.

"I wonder what finally convinced him to give up working." Victor mused aloud. "I thought I'd never live to see the day!"

Annette laughed softly at Victor's unintended joke. She believed that Mr. Prah would outlive them all and would still be working from a wheelchair in a hospice if it came to that.

She looked suspiciously at her husband at the other end of the banquet hall. He caught her gaze and gave her a curt nod. It was very unlike Mr. Prah to have let go of the reins of power. He had an ulterior motive, she was sure.

"Perhaps we're about to find out. He's getting up to the podium now," she answered Victor.

As the applause from the guests died down, Mr. Prah thanked them for coming and croaked on about how he had built his company from humble beginnings. He had started out as an ambitious boy carrying items on his own head to eventually build a logistics empire that had become the envy of other West African nations. It was a story that Annette had heard a thousand times and could retell line by line, using Mr. Prah's same rehearsed inflection.

But what Mr. Prah said next was in no way part of his traditional script.

"My wife and I have decided to set our sights elsewhere in Africa, and will spend the next year touring several countries, looking for new potential on the continent." He made grandiose gestures with his wrinkled hands. "We owe it to Africa to duplicate this kind of success everywhere. So you see friends, this is not the end of my journey as a businessman, but merely the beginning of a new chapter in the book of my life."

As the room erupted into raucous applause and cheers, Mr. Prah smiled smugly at Annette who was frozen in terror in her seat.

He knew. Somehow, he knew.

Afosua had spent the night curled up on the sofa in her living room. It creaked with relief as she rolled onto the floor. She dragged her aching body to the bathroom and doubled over the sink. When she glanced at her reflection in the mirror, she was startled by the haggard person staring back. Her eyes were blood red and dry white streaks lined her cheeks.

She had been crying in her sleep.

Afosua blew out a loud breath and prepared to take a long, hot shower before going in to work. On days like this, she was grateful that she worked with numbers. Numbers didn't have emotions. They didn't demand your opinion or ask you how you felt about the results. There were only wrong or right answers, no shades of truth in between. She would lock her office door and channel all her vacillating emotions into the sturdy world of mathematics.

As Afosua pushed open the glass doors leading into the offices of Phillips & Boakye, an earthy scent filled the air. Afosua took a deep breath in and dropped her briefcase by the receptionist's desk. Gertrude looked up and smiled and greeted her.

"Good morning, Gertrude. Is that coffee I smell?"

"I've just brewed some for the whole office," explained Gertrude, clearly satisfied with herself. "And a guest brought in some pastries for everyone this morning. I put them in the conference room."

Afosua didn't understand why the girl was so cheerful and didn't care, quite frankly. She hadn't planned on a sugary breakfast, but she felt compelled to indulge in some sort of pleasure this morning, no matter how small.

She swung the meeting room door open and made a beeline for the silver-rimmed pastry tray. She stopped just short of the table, overpowered by the scent of familiar cologne. Tony was sitting in the corner by the window, watching her stonily. His gall was more than she could stand.

"What are you doing here?" she hissed. "I thought I made myself very clear last night!"

Tony raised his eyebrows in surprise.

"I'm not here to see you," he said simply. He crossed his arms and matched her cold gaze with his.

"Oh please! Then who ARE you here to see? Gertrude perhaps?" she spat.

"Gertrude was and has always been nice enough to greet me with kindness in the morning, particularly in a professional setting," he said sternly. "Despite your assumptions, I'm not here on a romantic call, Ms. Gyemfi."

His formal tone corralled Afosua back into her right mind. He was right. This was the office, and there was a time and place for everything.

"Tony! You've brought chocolate scones, I see."

"Just like I do every year," Tony smiled. He stood up to shake the hand of Mark Phillips, the firm's CEO.

"Afosua, have you met Tony Coffie? Let me introduce you," Mark said congenially.

"We're... acquainted. Yes. I know Mr. Coffie," Afosua mumbled.

"Oh good! At some point I expect you'll be working closely with him. Tony has been handling our accounts for years. We contracted him because he's honest and probably the best in the business," Mark bellowed. His admiration for Tony was obvious.

Afosua nodded and managed a polite smile. Inside she felt sick. Where was the cool, confident demeanor she had spent years building up? Why would it flee her now?

"Yes... well if you'll excuse me, I have some catching up on some reports to do."

"Very good, Ms. Gyemfi," said Mark. "Would you shut the door behind you? As soon as Boakye comes in, we can begin."

Afosua closed the door behind her, muffling the sound of the two men laughing loudly. Would they eventually be laughing at her? Would Tony divulge in what way he 'knew' her? She decided not to care and charged into her office, yanking open her file cabinet and thumbing through her reports. Everything had been completed ahead of schedule... Everything except the mysterious and forbidden Swedish account.

As she sank into her chair, Afosua saw that Gertrude had brought in her purse and other belongings. She was grateful for the girl's thoughtfulness, which had inadvertently saved her from having to go out into the hallway and be confronted with the sound of Tony's voice. She tried to forget how physically close he was, or that she was pained by his dismissive attitude.

The sound of an alert on her phone broke Afosua's thoughts. She dug into the side pocket and fished it out. There was missed call from the night before.

Naa Akweley Blankson. Why on earth would she be calling?

Afosua steeled herself for a fight before re-dialing the number. Her call was answered on the third ring.

"Hello?" said a hollow female voice.

"Naa Akweley?" asked Afosua hesitantly.

The woman on the other end of the line didn't sound like the pretentious, snarling bulldog that she had come to know as First Lady Blankson.

"Yes..."

"It's Afosua. You called me last night. I never heard the phone ring -."

"It must have been an accident," Naa Akweley lied. "I must have called you by mistake."

Something in Naa Akweley's voice told Afosua that that was not true.

"Look, I may not know you very well, but I know you well enough to know that you don't make 'mistakes.'"

The mention of a mistake pushed Naa Akweley into hysterics. She began to sob uncontrollably on the other end of the line.

"Naa Akweley? Naa! Stop crying and tell me where you are."

"I'm – I'm at the beach… near the dunes."

"I'm coming right now."

*****

Afosua pulled into the rocky untarred parking lot and scanned the entrance of La Pleasure Beach. She didn't see Naa Akweley's car anywhere.

"She must have come by taxi," she muttered to herself.

After refusing to buy any of the decorated sea shells and beaded knick-knacks that sweaty young men were desperately trying to hawk, Afosua handed a bill to the toll worker and walked to the far end of the beach. The dunes were a largely deserted part of the shore that visitors rarely dared to venture towards because of the threat of being robbed by hooligans. Still, if Naa Akweley had taken the chance, Afosua would as well. The sand was cold beneath the soles of her feet, and the crisp morning ocean air sent a chill through her bones. The constriction of her grey pencil skirt made the walk even more difficult. Afosua grimaced as she sloshed through the small inlet that led into a lagoon filled with rubbish. Finally, she spotted a dark female figure in the distance.

"Naa Akweley," she breathed.

Afosua willed her legs to shuffle a little faster and managed a slow jog. Now gasping for breath, she tapped Naa Akweley on the shoulder and told her how glad she was to have found her. Naa Akweley never turned around. Hardly blinking, her eyes were fixed intently on something on the horizon. The sound of her shallow breathing was drowned by the noise of crashing ocean waves, mingling their salty spray with her tears.

"He only beats me on Monday's," Naa Akweley finally whispered. "Never on the weekends. It's too risky on the weekends. There's church on Sunday, after all… and Bible study on Wednesdays."

"Who beats you?"

Naa Akweley turned to look at Afosua, who covered her mouth in shock. Naa Akweley stared at her through a blackened, swollen left eye. Her keen nose and perfect cheek bones were riddled with tiny red crosses… imprints from Ian's pastor's ring.

"Normally it's a slap here, a shove there. But this time he went too far," whispered Naa Akweley.

Afosua was furious.

"No, Naa!" she raged. "The FIRST time he hit you he went too far."

Naa Akweley managed a weak smile and opened her mouth to say something, but no words found their way past her lips. Afosua's heart broke for her former foe as she clasped her hand in hers.

"Come on. You're coming home with me."

Naa Akweley was too weak to object. She didn't really want to. She squeezed Afosua's hand and leaned on her for support. The two women trudged away from the beach, their footprints eventually intertwining and forming a deep, single track in the sand.

******

It was 10:43 in the morning when Annette woke to the sounds of the gardener chopping down the hibiscus plant with his machete. She loved the vibrant color and the cheer that the plant brought to the garden, but Mr. Prah was allergic to its pollen and had it cut down every time the plant was in bloom. She wondered why he didn't simply uproot the bush altogether. Every season he ordered the branches to be cut back. It was as if he thrived on seeing beauty and promised destroyed in its prime.

As though in a trance, she rolled out of her bed, threw on a robe and slipped into her pink *chaley wote*. Mr. Prah should have left the house an hour ago to play squash or whatever it was he did with his mornings. She padded down the hallway towards the dining room, consoled only by the knowledge that she at least wouldn't have to face him, after his devastating announcement about their departure the evening before. Annette had hardly slept most of the night. Her thoughts were consumed by the consequences of what a move away from Accra would mean for her... and Sophia.

To her distress, Mr. Prah was seated at the dining room table having a late breakfast.

Damn.

"You look exhausted my dear." He peered at Annette over the brim of his newspaper with amusement.

"I didn't sleep that well."

"Something troubling you?"

"You know damned well what's troubling me!" she blurted. "If you had plans for us to travel you could have at least talked to me first!"

Mr. Prah huffed with disgust, mocking her.

"You're my wife – and I OWN you. I don't have to tell you a damned thing about my decisions," he spat.

Annette cast her eyes downward and crumpled onto a pea-green dining chair at the far end of the table, defeated. Mr. Prah hardly took any notice. He only spoke again when she had managed to compose herself and was pouring a cup of tea. This was their routine.

"My sources tell me you have been spending a lot of time with your seamstress."

Annette's heart threatened to leap out of her chest. Feeling lightheaded, she struggled to keep her breath steady. It wasn't working. She decided to stop breathing altogether. She lifted the cup of tea to her mouth, desperate to look unconcerned. Inside, she was a wreck.

"Now I ask myself... why would Annette be spending so much time with this woman?" Mr. Prah queried, as though he were piecing together a great mystery. "And the only answer I could come to is that you must be contemplating an affair."

Annette exhaled for the first time since he spoke. He suspected something, but he didn't know anything, at least not for certain.

"Whatever do you mean darling?" she asked feeling bolder. She sipped her tea nonchalantly.

"You know exactly what I mean! Why else would you be spending so much time with the seamstress unless you were building a wardrobe to attract the attentions of another man! I rarely see you in anything she's made."

Annette suddenly pitied Mr. Prah. His imagination was so limited. He could never dream that another woman had been sleeping with his wife.

"I told you before, my dear Mr. Prah – there is no other man that I am interested in. I'm not seeing another man, and…"

She paused before she spoke her next words, hoping that they wouldn't lead to her doom.

"…and I'm not going abroad with you."

Kwame Prah chuckled in disdain, as though someone had told him a tasteless joke. He put his newspaper back up against his face and spoke to her from behind the papyrus shield.

"We'll see about that my dear. We'll see about that."

*****

Naa Akweley was quiet for the majority of the car ride to Afosua's house, and Afosua didn't press her for conversation. She could only imagine what emotions the other woman might be suffering through, and she knew that at the moment all she could do was be as good a friend as possible, despite their difficult history.

When Naa Akweley finally did speak, her voice was pained and thin.

"It wasn't always like this you know."

Afosua glanced at her as she dodged a pothole in the road. She resisted the urge to curse, not wanting to offend her passenger.

"Ian used to be sweet, and kind… and so romantic," she whispered wistfully. "I remember the day I fell in love with him."

Afosua waited for her to continue, but Naa Akweley had closed her eyes and lost herself in the happier memories of her husband.

Naa Akweley was her father's favorite daughter and had been an unabashed *dadaba* when she was growing up. She had never understood her classmates' obsession with proving how difficult their lives were. They droned on about who had to weed the most compounds or walk the furthest to fetch the most water. What was the fun in that? She liked that she was much loved and appreciated by her parents, and reveled in how much they spoiled her. When her classmates teased her by calling her a daddy's girl, she surmised that they were just jealous and made it a point of telling them so.

As Ian pointed out a few weeks ago, Naa Akweley had never had to work a day in her life – but that was not something for which he could claim sole responsibility. Her father had seen to it that she'd always had the best of everything, and Ian discovered early that she expected a certain standard of living. It was with this knowledge in mind that he pursued her.

Naa Akweley and Ian met at a student-led church revival on campus when she was studying at Legon University. He had been handpicked by the student leadership to come give a word of encouragement to the student body for several reasons. Ian was uncommonly handsome. He was also a natural communicator who could manipulate the emotions of any audience with the mere nod of his head or lifting his voice. Naa Akweley was instantly smitten but she was not the only woman to notice that Ian was both attractive in articulation and physique. There was immediate talk among many of the 'Krife' campus girls of divine revelations and visions that Ian was their husband. Most promptly set about trying to convince Ian of this sacred insight during the long nights of evening prayer. But out of all the women who thronged those meetings, Ian's eyes locked on Naa Akweley's and he chose *her*.

For the next few months they were inseparable. When her classes took her away from him she thought her world would end. Order would only be restored when she saw him again. Eventually Naa Akweley stopped going to her classes altogether, choosing to sit in on the lectures Ian had to attend or waiting for him outside of his classes when his professors would not let her in. It was only a matter of time before she submitted herself to him fully.

The first night they lay together, Ian seemed shocked by the resistance to his penetration.

"You're a virgin?"

Naa Akweley nodded in uncomfortable confirmation, wondering if being with Ian like this was all wrong or if this was her fault. Had she seduced this man whose heart harkened after God? Everything they had been taught spoke against pre-marital sex, and yet there they were in the bed of his dorm room. Seeing the doubt in her eyes, Ian stroked her head assuredly and promised to go slow. She was amazed at how alive she felt when he was in her, filling her up. She wanted this feeling forever.

Eight months after they'd met, Ian approached Naa Akweley's father to seek his approval for their marriage. Her father flatly refused, calling Ian a charlatan. He was too good looking and too smooth. When Naa Akweley begged her father to reconsider, he wouldn't hear of it.

"Naa, sweetheart. This boy will ruin you," her father cautioned. "You love him far more than he loves you, and that's a bad place for a girl to be. Believe me... I'm a man, and I know."

Naa Akweley could not accept her father's rejection, and when he saw he was making no headway he forced her to make a heavy choice.

"You will have to choose Ian or choose your family. If you go with him, no one from this house will ever speak to you again!"

The next morning Naa Akweley packed her bags and set off to start her new life. Her father refused to come outside to see her off and her mother wept as though the waiting taxi was carrying Naa Akweley to her own funeral. That was the last day she saw her family. Those were also the last days of true happiness she would ever know. She tried not to live with regret over the choices she had made, but it was so hard.

"We're here," said Afosua, dragging Naa Akweley back into the present.

Afosua sprinted to the passenger's side of the car and took Naa Akweley's hand. The woman looked like a terrified lamb, and it scared her. She had never seen a woman so broken, not even when she had looked at her own reflection in the mirror a few years before when her own world had come crashing down around her ears.

Afosua called for the house-girl to bring her some fresh hand towels to clean Naa Akweley up with.

"Just set them down there please, Joyce," she directed.

Joyce lingered in the room, unsure about what she was seeing.

"Ah... Sister Afosua. Is that not..."

Afosua silenced her with a warning glare.

"Never mind who that is! You can go back and continue what you were doing. I'm sure my mother needs you for something."

Joyce was stung by Afosua's severity and wordlessly left the room. It suddenly dawned on Afosua that it was going to be difficult to keep Naa Akweley's presence in her home a secret for long. With so famous a husband and with pictures of the couple plastered on billboards all over Accra, Naa Akweley would be instantly recognizable. For the moment, this wasn't a major concern, Afosua thought ruefully. Ian had done quite a number on Akweley's face; she hardly looked like herself.

"Have some ice-water, Naa," Afosua offered.

Naa Akweley settled herself slowly into a plush armchair and took a sip. Her pregnant belly did not look quite as large as it had a few weeks ago. Afosua wondered if that was normal, but decided not to pry. One thing at a time. She went to her medicine cabinet and retrieved some antiseptic for Naa Akweley's bruises and some cocoa butter to soothe her. As Afosua rubbed her tense shoulders she was surprised at how willing Naa Akweley was to submit to the tender touch of someone whom she had just recently claimed to hate. Perhaps this was some odd twist of nature. After all, she had just been pummeled by someone who was supposed to love her. The two women sat in silence, with only the scent of cocoa butter and the sounds of their ragged breathing filling the air.

When Naa Akweley seemed a little more relaxed, Afosua relaxed her grip on her shoulders and tried to offer some words of comfort.

"You can stay as long as you like, and we can figure out what to do for the future."

"Okay. Thank you," Naa Akweley replied quietly.

Afosua was unsure about what to do next; so she did what came naturally to her. She prepared to flee.

"I left work suddenly, so I'll have to get back," she explained, gathering her keys. "If you need anything, just call for Joyce. She will help you while I'm gone."

"Afosua... wait," Naa Akweley begged. "I could really use someone to talk to. I heard about what happened to you all those years ago. Would you talk to me please? Would you tell me how you made it out? I – I need some hope right now."

Afosua gripped her keys tighter and stood frozen at the door. Naa Akweley was asking her to reopen a casket that she had sealed shut ages ago. She wasn't entirely sure she wanted to revisit the memories it contained, even if it meant saving the life of this woman. The woman Naa Akweley was referring to was dead, and Afosua wanted to keep it that way.

*****

Annette's car squealed helplessly under the stress of racing and braking. All she could think of was Sophia, and how quickly she had to get to her house. She had left Mr. Prah sitting at their table with a smirk on his face, after telling her that she had no choice but to go anywhere he demanded.

"You have no family, and no friends except the ones I permit. Where do you think you can go?" he challenged.

Annette could only think of one place.

Little children in their school uniforms milled along the side of the road, impeding her progress. She had to brake abruptly more than once to avoid hitting a child who had wandered too close to the edge of the street. When she finally got to Sophia's gate, there was an unfamiliar car parked in front of the house. Annette paid little attention to it and quickly greeted Idrisu before going up to see her lover.

"Madam! Please she has a visitor!" he called after her.

She ignored him and burst into the front door.

"Sophia!"

A man in dark trousers and a white traditional shirt was sitting on Annette's favorite chair while Sophia was leaning on the wall. Her arms were folded across her chest, a scowl written across her face. Annette had interrupted their conversation.

"Annette… what are you doing here?" Sophia was surprised to see her. They were not supposed to meet until later that evening.

"I had to come and see you," Annette breathed, "it's very urgent."

Sophia moved in a little closer and sat down next to the man on the chair.

"Annette, please meet my husband – John. He just flew in from Nigeria."

A pit grew in Annette's stomach and she felt a tingle between her legs. She was about to urinate on herself out of sheer anxiety. Fortunately, she had just enough presence of mind to not embarrass herself so completely.

"I – I see," she stammered. She reached out to shake his hand, which he took heartedly.

"Nice to meet you Annette," he said warmly. "You are even more beautiful than Sophia described."

 Annette was confused.

"Sophia… can I speak to you alone please?"

"We can talk in front of my husband," replied Sophia. "We have no secrets."

Annette bristled.

"Please? I really need to talk to you alone."

John nodded his consent and Sophia led Annette into the back room. Annette began to whisper loudly.

"What do you mean 'you have no secrets'? And what do you mean 'your husband'? Since when have you been married? Does he know about us?!"

Annette was already beyond consolation, and the surreptitiously delivered news of a husband was dealing a fresh barrage of blows to all of her senses. She thought the room was collapse on her. It would be better if it did. Sophia pulled Annette in close, rubbing the small of her back until she calmed down.

"Of course he doesn't know about us, you silly girl," she scolded. "What African man do you know would be okay with his wife sleeping with another woman? He knows you're a dedicated client, that's all."

Annette's pounding heart finally began to slow down. She hugged Sophia tightly, pressing her body against hers and kissing her hungrily.

"We can't do that right now," Sophia said harshly. "He's in the next room!"

"Sophia, Mr. Prah is taking me away," Annette wailed desperately. "He's taking me away from Accra for a whole year... maybe even more! I'm going to leave him."

"Leave him and go where?"

"I was hoping to stay with you..."

Sophia scoffed at the idea.

"That, my dear, is impossible."

Annette was wounded. She had been sure Sophia would welcome her with no reservations.

"What do you mean impossible? We love each other. I love YOU. I tell you all the time!"

"And when have you heard me say I love you back?" Sophia challenged. "I know you love me, yes, but I've never confessed to loving you."

"But for the last three years..."

"For the last three years I've been fucking your brains out because you're a woman whose husband's dick is at risk of falling off as we speak," Sophia spat. "I pitied you, and you mistook pity for love. But I can't pity you enough to let you stay here and ruin my reputation. I have too much at stake"

"So that's it then?" Annette sobbed. "This is how it ends? It's alright for you to fuck me in secret, but when it matters you just give up? "

"I'm afraid so, my dear," Sophia said, stepping aside and showing Annette the door. "This is Africa, and we are not living in a fairy tale. Good bye and take care."

Annette's woeful display ceased immediately and she wiped her face vigorously. She would spare no more tears for this callous woman. She charged out of Sophia's house and went back to face Mr. Prah and her doom. Sophia was right. Her life was not a fairy tale. She cursed the day she had dared to fall in love.

*****

Afosua dropped her keys on the coffee table and sat wearily on a foot stool. She would be forced to re-open Pandora's Box, as painful as it was.

"What have you heard?" she asked Naa Akweley.

"That you left your husband. That he dehumanized you. That you were unfit... there were so many rumors."

Afosua nodded.

"All that is true," she confessed. "Except he wasn't my husband; we never made it down the aisle, although God knows I wanted to."

Naa Akweley sat silently and waited. Afosua took a deep breath.

"I will tell you what happened, but after this we will never speak of it again. Okay?"

"Okay."

****

It was supposed to be a lazy Sunday morning, but Afosua's body was damp with sweat, her throat was hoarse and she was about to cum for the third time. As she dipped her back, Ahmed Laiche's penetration become deeper and more insistent from behind. In just 36 hours, she would be Mrs. Afosua Laiche. She loved the ring of her name to-be, as well as the ring that her fiancé had given her. As the diamond on her left hand caught a glimpse of the dawn light filtering through the window, her climax came quickly and suddenly. Feeling her pulsate, Ahmed groaned and finally had his release. He refused to cum unless Afosua did first.

"You really made me work hard for that one." Ahmed kissed her on the neck and nuzzled into her shoulder.

"I'm sorry. I was a little distracted."

"And how could you be distracted with all this dick drilling you?" He laughed.

Afosua scolded mockingly, "Don't talk dirty!"

"You know you like it." Ahmed trailed the palm of his hand down Afosua's back and cupped her buttocks. They were so hungry for each other that their passion defied all responsibility. Still, Afosua knew that they had a busy day ahead and they had to get up.

"I'm going to take a shower," she whispered. "We have to finish up our last minute plans."

"Fine. If you insist," Ahmed sulked. "If it were up to me, we'd just go to the justice and get our license drawn up. No party, no reception, none of that foolishness."

Afosua knew exactly where Ahmed stood on the subject of a wedding celebration. Being from Algeria, he was accustomed to weddings being a weeklong affair, just as she was as a Ghanaian. He was a simple man and wanted no part of any such affair. Afosua wouldn't have minded simplicity, too, but she knew that Ahmed's mother would accuse her of trying to steal one more piece of happiness from her by refusing to have a proper wedding. It was simply easier to appease that woman. After weeks of begging and bribing, Afosua had gotten her future husband to agree to a small ceremony and reception. She kissed him one final time before stepping into a stream of hot water.

As Afosua washed her hair, she recalled the first time she'd met Ahmed two years before. It was in their third year of university and they were taking the same differential equations course. The course wasn't a requirement to graduate, but she had a few credit hours to spare and she wanted to do it for fun. There were seven students in the class; Afosua was the only Black female. She stood out like an ant in a bowl of sugar. No one ever made her feel unwelcome, though, and by the end of the first semester all seven of the undergraduates had become very close. They studied regularly together and met up for lunch when their schedules permitted. Out of the entire bunch, Ahmed Laiche was the most reserved. He was scrawny with thick curly hair and hazel colored eyes that were always watching. Afosua found this alarming – and alluring.

"How come you don't talk as much as everyone else?" Afosua interrogated him one day when they were in the library alone.

"Well for one thing, this is a library and it's a place that demands silence," he quipped.

Afosua chuckled quietly.

"And why are you always so chatty," he asked her in return.

"I don't know," she mused. "I guess it's my culture. We just like to talk a lot I guess."

"It seems like a quality that a person who was always seeking approval might possess."

Afosua bristled. "I wouldn't say that, I wouldn't classify myself as an attention seeker."

"I didn't say you were an attention seeker. And I'd still be careful if I were you. You come off as very trusting. People lie, but numbers never do."

This was the most that Afosua had ever heard Ahmed speak, to her or anyone else. She stared at him for a good moment, until this compelled him to speak again.

"I like your hair," he said pensively.

"What?"

"I like your hair. I like the way its color changes when it catches the light."

Afosua beamed. She was genuinely pleased with the compliment, although she didn't see what he was talking about. Her hair was plain black and wasn't much different from any other Ghanaian woman's hair either.

"No one's ever told me that before," she smiled. "That was really sweet... I could almost kiss you!"

She was laughing but Ahmed took her seriously.

"Why don't you then?"

"Eh?"

"Kiss me."

Afosua was surprised by his candor, but acquiesced all the same. What harm could it do? She leaned in and prepared to give Ahmed a peck on the cheek. He slid his hand behind the back of her neck, trapping her and pulling her towards him, seeking something more. His lips were so soft, his breath so sweet. They would have kissed longer if she had not reminded herself that they were in the library and pulled away – but that moment sealed them forever.

They were inseparable after that. Soon, they stopped studying with the group and went off to study on their own; taking breaks between solving equations to make love in the solitude of the lab or to pleasure each other discreetly if there were other people around. They moved in together right after graduation, and within a few months Ahmed grew from a shy skinny student to a well-built man, thanks to a new steady diet of good food and great sex. Their lives became the stuff of perfect romance novels. Not only did each of them land good jobs right out of university, they had found unbridled love and friendship with each other so young in life.

But just like every fairy tale, there had to be a villain: Ahmed's mother despised Afosua. The recollection of Asma Laiche's hatred for her snapped Afosua back into the present.

After she toweled off, Afosua smacked Ahmed on the thigh to force him out of bed.

"Come on, babes," she pleaded. "I don't want to be late for our rehearsal dinner. I don't need another reason to make your mother angry with me."

"I don't know why you care some much. It's not like you're marrying her."

"I know that baby, but it's just so much easier when your mother-in-law likes you, and I really want us to get along. All of us."

Ahmed grunted and skulked towards the shower.

Ahmed never said much about his family, except that he was the 'runt of the litter.' With four older brothers, he was accustomed to being ignored and to his accomplishments being overlooked. Most young men like Ahmed would have taken advantage of this neglect and gotten into mischief, but it had only made Ahmed draw further into himself. It wasn't until he met Afosua that he'd come out of his shell. He was more confident when she was around; she made him believe he could do anything.

Just as Ahmed was about to step into the shower, he turned around to discover that Afosua had slipped into a pair of black lace panties and a matching bra.

"Did you put those on for me?"

"Yes. For later."

"How about for now?"

"Oh come on," she scoffed. You can't recover that quickly!"

He ignored her and guided her to the floor with a mischievous smirk. With one hand he slipped off Afosua's panties and with the other he roughly pushed her legs open. Afosua leaned back reluctantly as he kissed her labia. When his tongue found her clitoris, she gave up resisting.

"Ahmed we're going to be late. Ahmed... Ahmed!"

"Shhh....," he ordered.

Oh, well. What harm would a few more minutes do?

****

It was a half hour ride from London to Croydon. There were some gifts in three village shops that Afosua wanted to buy for the guests, and she had to go see about the venue. When Ahmed and Afosua arrived at *Evelyn's Events*, the company coordinating their wedding, they were 20 minutes late and Asma was already there. She was not happy.

"I see that the two of you decided to show up," she snarled. "This isn't Africa, Afosua. In England we stick to our time."

"It wasn't Afosua's fault, Ummi," said Ahmed, pulling Afosua close. "And is Algeria not part of Africa?"

Asma Laiche scowled. She hated it when her son would point this out, as though two countries sharing the same continental land mass made this monkey her equal or, better still, worthy of her son.

Sensing tension, the event planner stepped in.

"Let's get started, shall we?"

"Lead the way," said Afosua.

Everything was in order, and it was going to be a beautiful ceremony, the planner gushed. Afosua and Ahmed had chosen turquoise and burnt orange as their wedding colors, which were non-traditional and striking. Even Asma approved. The caterers would set everything up and Evelyn's staff would handle all the other details. Now, all that was left to get out of the way was the rehearsal dinner and to be finally married in the morning. Although things were unpleasant between Afosua and the elder Mrs. Laiche, she was still grateful that so much else was going right. The forecast called for warm spring weather, and there wouldn't be a cloud in the sky all week. She hoped it would be an omen for her and Ahmed's future together.

Sensing her thoughts, he came behind her and hugged her tightly.

"Come on. Let's go to dinner," he whispered. "I want to get all these ridiculous steps out of the way if it'll get me closer to marrying you."

She smiled and leaned back to kiss him.

"I love you."

"I love you too."

****

There should have been 20 guests at the rehearsal dinner. All of Ahmed's brothers had come, but his father was unable to make it. Afosua glanced at the empty seat and wondered what would have been so pressing as to keep the old man from his son's nuptials. She knew better than to ask. Ahmed never gave explanations about his family. He was not particularly close to them, but in time Afosua hoped they would all learn to get along – perhaps even love each other. She had never had a big family of her own, and she was about to marry into one. She wished Ahmed would make a better effort to reconnect.

"You look amazing," Ahmed whispered as soon as they were seated.

Afosua brushed her lips against his neck and whispered her thanks. The strapless jewel toned dress Afosua was wearing was a last-minute find, and it complimented her brown skin so perfectly that she couldn't let it go. Afosua felt confident, beautiful and loved. It was one of the happiest nights of her life.

She took a break from chatting with her friends who had come down for the wedding to speak to Asma.

"I hope you're having a nice time," she said warmly.

Asma stared at her icily.

"As good a time as one could have at such a cheap event," she hissed. "This is not the way we are married in our culture."

"I know," Afosua admitted, trying to remain calm. "But this is the way Ahmed wanted it. If it were left to him, we would have eloped."

The revelation seemed to shock Asma, and a strange look came over her face. Afosua didn't have time to figure out what the matter was, because she and Ahmed were being called to the stage to be given a toast. She excused herself quickly.

Everyone from their small class in university where they had met had come to give their congratulations.

"Maybe this marriage will finally be the beginning of African unity," quipped a friend, eliciting chuckles from the crowd.

When everyone had had their say, Ahmed's elder brother took the mic, though he didn't need it. Rafiq Laiche was an enormous man with a booming voice. You could see and hear him coming from 10 miles away.

"I don't think anyone was more shocked at this union than I was," he began. "When I heard that Ahmed was getting married, I wondered 'Who would marry such a scrawny, awkward kid?' Then I heard he was engaged to a black girl from West Africa and it all made sense. She must be used to people looking as though they are starving."

The room grew deathly silent. Someone had sucked all of the oxygen out of it.

Rafiq turned and looked at Ahmed.

"You can do so much better than this little black cunt. Why do you think Ammi is not here today? He would not see you willingly mix our blood with this monkey. They are okay for sex, but certainly not for marriage, Ahmed."

Afosua stared at Ahmed, waiting for him to throttle his brother, or at the very least come to her defense. He just stood there... stood there silently like a man trapped in a stockade. Maybe he was ashamed of her. Maybe that's why he never took her around his family. Maybe this was all wrong.

Afosua burst into tears and fled from the packed room that had been filled with so much warmth just a few minutes ago. She couldn't shake the chill that was taking over her body. Ahmed raced after her and caught up with her in the tree-lined courtyard outside of the cottage they had rented for the dinner.

"Why didn't you say something?" she wailed. "Why didn't you defend me?!"

"Afosua... I'm sorry!" Ahmed was panicking.

"Am I so cheap that you don't even think I'm worth protecting?"

"Sweetheart – you know that's not true!"

Something occurred to her. Something Ahmed had never mentioned before.

"You might have warned me that your family was a pack of roving racists. Here I was thinking that your mother didn't like me because I was taking away one of her sons, something Freudian or simple as that." She laughed acerbically when she said her next words. "Turns out she's just got a problem with my blackness!"

Ahmed was silent.

"So it's true then? And you've known all along!"

"Baby," Ahmed said pleadingly, "my family is a bunch of idiots. There, I said it. But why do you think I've stayed away from them all these years? It's because I don't think like that. I love you!"

Afosua felt her throat tighten.

"No you don't, Ahmed," she croaked. "Love doesn't behave this way. Love wouldn't run away from a fight. If this is the way we're going to start our lives... I think it's safe to assume that you don't love me – and maybe I can't love you."

She turned to leave the courtyard but Ahmed caught her by the arm.

"Don't leave like this. Don't leave *me*."

His hazel eyes yielded a stream of tears. Afosua had never seen him so broken. She almost relented, but the sting of what had just transpired stopped her from giving in to heart's desire to forgive him.

"Goodbye, Ahmed."

Afosua began the quick walk back to the hotel room, leaving her stunned lover and the setting sun behind her.

Just before she got to the hotel, a car black screeched up beside her.

"Want a lift?" said an unfamiliar voice.

Before she could reply, a hand went over her mouth and a man's arm pulled into the vehicle.

"Not a word," he breathed into her ear.

In an instant, someone put a piece of duct tape over her mouth and a bag over her head. The last thing she saw before the abduction was the lobby of the hotel. As the car sped off, the sounds of the city grew fainter and fainter. She was in total dread of what might happen next.

When the car finally stopped, Afosua was pushed out onto the ground. Rafiq whipped the bag off of her head, laughing maniacally at her bewildered expression.

"You almost got away with it, huh?" he sneered. "A little African bastard like you thought she was going to weasel her way into our family? I don't think so."

He kicked her twice in the stomach as she lay helplessly on the ground.

"Oh yes, we did our research," he continued, pummeling her with his heavy fists on every other word. "I know that you're an illegitimate child, that your mother was a whore, that you are NOTHING. My parents deserve better than to allow dirt into our family."

Afosua was unable to speak, but she glowered at her assaulter, hoping her eyes conveyed how much hatred she had for him. Someone was holding her arms behind her, preventing her from fighting back. Seeing that her will was not yet broken, Rafiq continued to kick and punch Afosua for what seemed like an eternity. Finally, after taking the only beating Afosua had ever received in her life, she finally stopped moving. There was no more resistance left in her. As her head slumped into her chest, Rafiq stepped away from her.

He stomped towards the car, but paused and then turned around. He signaled to the stranger who had come with him.

"Lift her up and spread her open."

Rafiq tore off Afosua's gown, pushed three of his fingers into her vagina and raped her savagely. Afosua writhed and twisted her body in pain, her muffled screams barely audible. Rafiq snorted.

"So this is the magical pussy that took my brother out of his senses."

He laughed maliciously and ripped her engagement ring off her hand.

"Drop her."

Afosua hit the ground with a thud and except for the ragged heaving of her chest, didn't move again. Rafiq knelt beside her and whispered a warning into her ear.

"If you contact the police, I will kill you. And if you try to contact Ahmed, I will kill him."

The world instantly went black.

*****

When Afosua awoke, she was in a hospital and a nurse was bringing in a tray of medication. She was surprised to see Afosua awake.

"You've been asleep a long time."

The nurse was a pretty brunette with a crooked tooth. It was the first thing Afosua noticed when she smiled.

"Where am I?" she whispered.

"You're safe, my dear. A farmer found you early this morning and brought you in. Good thing too. You were lucky that you weren't exposed to the elements for longer, seeing as how you were brought in…"

Afosua looked at the nurse quizzically. A flood of memories hit her suddenly. She had been brought in naked and abused. She was so ashamed.

Realizing her mistake, the nurse spoke quickly and tried to sound cheerful.

"The doctor will be in soon to see you though! He can talk to you about everything. It looks like you're going to recover just nicely."

The nurse was young, in her 20s perhaps, and hadn't gained enough experience to be an adept liar.

"What aren't you telling me?" Afosua demanded.

"I think we should wait for –"

"Tell me!" she shouted.

The nurse stalled but finally revealed the truth. It might be easier to swallow if it came from another woman, she reckoned, so she stumbled through an explanation.

"My dear… I'm so sorry for your loss. There was a baby… I mean, a fetus! You were a little less nine weeks along – but because of the trauma to your abdomen…"

The nurse's voice trailed off and Afosua deduced the rest. Rafiq had killed her baby, Ahmed's baby.

As she mourned the child she never knew she was going to have, two detectives walked in to question Afosua. Inevitably, they asked the question that she had been dreading.

"Do you know who did this to you, Ms. Gyemfi?"

She shook her head 'no' and looked out the window.

"Is there anyone we can call?" said one officer. He gestured at her left hand, which still bore a faint tan line of the ring she had been wearing for months.

Who could she call? Her parents were in Ghana and to call Ahmed would be his doom.

"No," she said. "There is no one you can call. I am all alone."

It was true.

******

Naa Akweley had no words to console Afosua, who tried to tell her story with as much candor as she could muster. Even to that day, her loss was too much for Afosua to really grapple with.

"I'm so sorry, Afosua," Naa Akweley murmured softly. "Whatever happened next?"

A dry laugh escaped Afosua's lips.

"A year later I left Croydon when I felt braver and went back to London. And I did see Ahmed again, by chance on the tube. He was with somebody else; and she was wearing my ring." She smiled ruefully. "I left for Ghana soon after that."

Naa Akweley felt a deep sense of shame wash over her.

"I have treated you so unfairly," she confessed. "That's not what I heard at all. I heard that –"

Afosua held up her hand to stop her.

"Please spare me the details from the gossip mill," she interjected. "I can only imagine what people have come up with. The truth is hard enough to deal with."

Naa Akweley nodded. She understood.

Afosua got up to leave. It was late and the office would be closing soon, but she didn't want to stay in the room where so much pity lingered. There were many things she could handle, but pity was not one of them.

"Remember, ring for Joyce if you need anything."

Naa Akweley nodded again. Moments later, she watched Afosua's car pull quickly out of the driveway. No matter how fast Afosua ran, she could never overtake the hurtful memories of her past.

Annette drove around Accra in a daze for hours. Stunned by Sophia's unrepentant revelation that she was married and the harshness with which she had delivered the news, Annette sought solace in food. Frankie's Ice Cream shop was across the street from Sophia's studio, and whenever she was unable to see Sophia, Annette would sit in the window of the restaurant to stare wistfully at the store window. She ate her ice-cream absently until the buzz and hum of evening traffic snapped her out of her trance. She would have to go back home and deal with her life. Sitting here wasn't going to solve anything.

When she got home, Mr. Prah was lounging in the living room, reading a newspaper as usual.

"Oh. You're finally home," he snickered.

"Yes."

"Come sit by me," he commanded.

Annette mechanically did as she was told. Mr. Prah held her by the neck and looked searchingly into her eyes. Where had she been?

"Mr. Prah... darling. It dawned on me today that I truly have nowhere to go. I have no one but you," Annette said, choking back her emotions. "You've created a world for me, and I have no choice but to live in it."

Mr. Prah smiled.

"And don't you ever forget it," he whispered maliciously.

With his free hand, he removed his penis from his trousers and pushed Annette's head towards his lap. She began to suck robotically. Mr. Prah leaned back and groaned, leaving Annette's mouth full of his semen and her tears.

*****

Afosua felt emotionally drained when she got back into the office. Everyone was gone, and she was happy for the solitude. She hadn't done any work today, dealing with Naa Akweley and going down the dark path of those memories from so many years ago but physically, she felt like she had been laboring in a field like all day. She was exhausted and she was sad.

After her PC powered up Afosua began to type furiously. The algorithm she was working on was failing to solve the fiscal dilemma her newest client was facing. DeutschTech Laboratories was a German company that had an expressed interest in coming to Ghana to investigate *synsepalum dulcificum* or 'asaa', as it was known locally. The plant is native to West Africa and the German company was trying to exploit its benefits for German clients. At least that's how Afosua saw it and she convinced herself that she didn't care. Mark Phillips had made her the team lead on this project, and the financial windfall Phillips & Boakye stood to gain from its success was all she was focused on. This was her shot at the recognition she knew she deserved. When Afosua looked back through the columns of her spreadsheet, she realized what the problem was. Some of the terms had not been translated from German to English. Gertrude would have to fix that in the morning.

Afosua leaned back in her swivel chair and sighed. She hated waiting on other people to get her work done, but there was nothing more to be done at this hour. She closed her eyes and wondered what she would do next. The sound of her door creaking made them fly open in panic. She thought she was alone!

"Why are you here so late?"

"Tony?"

She was bewildered by his presence.

"What are you doing here at all?"

"I have an office on the other side of the building."

"Since when?" she challenged.

"Since always," he chuckled. "You forget that I have been working for P&B long before you got here."

That was true. Afosua let her guard down. Tony was so nice, and she had no reason to be a bitch to him. Now that Mr. Phillips had made it clear that they were going to be working together, she may as well extend an olive branch.

"Tony, I want to apologize for the way I acted a few days ago," she said. "You were such a gentleman, and I was –"

"A total bitch?"

Afosua stiffened. Tony saw immediately that he had offended her, and offered his own apology.

"I think we're about equal now, as far as hurt feelings and apologies go," he said. "Can we start from the beginning?"

"Of course," Afosua said smiling. "How about we start with a proper introduction?"

She held out her hand to shake his.

"Good evening. My name is Afosua Gyemfi, and I'm an actuary for Phillips & Boakye."

"Tony Coffie, roaming accountant" he laughed. "And I think I was just as happy with the nature of our first introduction."

His grip on Afosua's hand tightened and he pulled her in close to him. His broad chest felt warm and hard through his shirt. Afosua held her breath.

"I think this is where we left off the last time I was in here," Tony murmured, unbuttoning her blouse.

With one hand Afosua undid his belt and slid her hand down his zipper. He was rock hard. Within moments they were naked and he was on top of her, thrusting with urgency and willing her to cum. When she did, Tony refused to cease his penetration and buried his head into her chest, licking and biting her nipples until they were erect and wet from his kisses. When she screamed and came again, he finally released as well. Realizing what he had done, Tony looked at Afosua with panic in his eyes. His wanton passion had taken over his sense of responsibility. Afosua rubbed his neck reassuringly and pulled him back on top of her. She whispered that it was okay. Everything was okay. Unsure, he lay back down anyway, thumbing her clitoris and running his soft lips over her cheek. Afosua listened to the steady ticking of the second hand on the clock in the hallway, comforted by the predictability of time as it passed.

There would be no conception – no baby. Rafiq had robbed her of that long ago.

*****

When Mr. Prah finally released her, Annette ran to her room and vomited in the sink. She hated the very smell of that miserable old man, and the memory of his penis in her mouth was more than she could bear. Was this the way her life was going to be forever? Groveling and scraping and obeying the old toad's every command? Annette had already suffered so many years under his tyrannical rule and decided that she had had enough.

There was ₵50,000 locked away in box that Annette had been saving for years. Part of that was money she owed Sophia for a dress she had just commissioned, but there was no way Annette was going to pay her now. It wasn't a lot, but it was hers and Mr. Prah had no idea about it. Annette hastily formulated a plan of escape, biting her lip until it bled as her strategy came into focus. With trembling hands she packed a few clothes into an oversized bag and grabbed the money. When the house was still and the bullfrogs began croaking, she left through the back gate of the estate, disappearing into the night.

When Gertrude arrived at work the next morning, there was an email from Afosua informing her that she needed her to finish up a translation for the DeutschTech project. Gertrude didn't mind the work; it was the hurried, dismissive tone of the email she didn't care for. She shrugged off her irritation and set out to finish the translation.

Gertrude was of mixed race, but you wouldn't know it to look at her at her first glance. She found out when she was eight years old that her father was white, but she had never met him. Her mother was the maid for a German family that had lived in Ghana years ago. Gertrude's birth was the result of a brief dalliance between her and her 'master.' All Gertrude knew was that her father worked for an engineering group that was overseeing a water project in some village, and that soon after her mother discovered she was pregnant the family returned to Germany. Gertrude imagined that her mother would have been repulsed by anything Germany had to offer given the result of her previous circumstances, but the woman scrimped, saved and did without for years to make sure that Gertrude got a decent education and became fluent German, courtesy of the Goethe Institute. As a teenager, Gertrude resented the extra hours she had to spend studying a new language, but when Phillips & Boakye announced that they were hiring only bi-lingual candidates for their organization, she was grateful for those grueling hours and missed playtimes.

No one at Phillips & Boakye knew about her humble origins, however, and she planned to keep it that way.

Mark Phillips poked his head out of his office door and smiled at her.

"Gertrude," he said, "when Ms. Gyemfi comes in, will you have her join us in the conference room?"

"Yes. Of course."

"And please stay when she comes. I'd like you to sit in on this meeting."

Gertrude's heart skipped a beat. She had never been asked to sit in on a meeting with either of the owners. She usually had to man the front desk just in case a client called. She wondered what it meant. Suddenly her heart froze in terror. She was going to be fired. She had violated the company's IT rule by going on social media sites during work hours and she was going to be fired. She didn't have time to come up with an explanation because Afosua walked in at that moment, looking happier than Gertrude had seen her in weeks.

"Mr. Boakye and Mr. Phillips would like to see you in the meeting room, Ms. Gyemfi."

Afosua's smile immediately faded. Had someone found out she had just violated the office rules by having sex on the floor? She resisted the urge to panic.

"Tell them I'll be right in. Let me go and grab a note pad."

Afosua tossed her belongings on to a swivel chair in her office and cursed under her breath. She walked bravely into the meeting room with Gertrude.

"Ladies! Please have a seat," said Mark Phillips. "We have a few things to discuss."

Gertrude looked over at Harold Boakye, who unlike Mark was scowling and staring at the pair of them with cold eyes.

"DeutschTech has asked us to come to Germany to consult on the *asaa* project," Mark smiled. "They are so impressed with what we've done so far that they've accepted our bid to be their primary actuary. However, they do recognize the risks involved when translating from one language to another, and they want to eliminate those risks by having us come and meet their team in person."

Afosua and Gertrude both loosened their respective grips on their chairs and nodded congenially. Gertrude began furiously scribbling notes. She was sure that Robert would need them for the trip. He was always sent on trips abroad.

"This has huge benefits and implications for everyone in this room," Mark continued. "This is a real chance for Phillips & Boakye to shine. *Synsepalum dulcificum* has immense potential as a dietary supplement, possibly even as a treatment for diabetic ailments. There are billions of dollars at stake for Deutsch and for us in commission, if they are successful."

"That is why I would rather have a man on this project," Harold Boakye interjected. "As Mark said, there is much at risk."

Afosua and Gertrude remained silent and did not address the sexist remark. Neither wanted to get into it with Mr. Boakye. As expected, Mr. Phillips came to their defense.

"Ms. Gyemfi, this is your opportunity to show real leadership in the company," he said, smiling at Afosua. "And I want you to work on this with someone you can get along with, whom you can bounce ideas off and, more importantly, who possesses a skill that no one else in this office has – the ability to speak German."

Gertrude stopped writing and stared at Mr. Phillips. He was smiling at her.

"Wait. What? Me? I'm going?"

"Unfortunately, yes," sneered Mr. Boakye. "I would rather have Robert or one of the other senior analysts accompany Ms. Gyemfi on this trip, but Mark makes a compelling point: You *are* fluent in German, and you will be able to read between the lines of what is said in any discussion. It will strengthen our advantage."

"And having too many people on one trip will be a distraction," added Mr. Phillips. "Being distracted is NOT to our advantage."

Gertrude didn't bother to stop herself from beaming. She was finally going to get a chance to make something of herself. She was one step closer to erasing the memory of her past.

"When do we leave?" asked Afosua.

"Next week," said Mr. Phillips. "Gertrude, if you don't have a passport, go ahead and make an appointment to have one expedited. Thank you ladies, that is all."

Afosua strode into her office to prepare presentations and gather data. Gertrude sat forlornly at her desk and looked for the number to the Ghana Immigration Service. Her reverie was dulled by the sudden recollection that she had never been outside of Ghana... never at all. Now was not the time, she told herself! She straightened her spine and fought the old urge to feel sorry for herself because she was the underprivileged child of a maid, and then she dialed the number.

*****

Annette had walked for most of the night after she fled Mr. Prah's house. There were few taxis in the area after sunset, since most people who lived in Trasacco Valley had cars of their own. She didn't dare go by the Tema Motorway, because it was too well lit and someone might recognize her. She didn't dare fall asleep in one of the many abandoned kiosks because she might be robbed or worse. After ducking every time she saw a car pass by, Annette finally approached a taxi rank at dawn and chartered a ride to Asylum Down.

Asylum Down wasn't exactly a slum, but it certainly wasn't a place where people of wealth frequented either. She knew that she would be safe there. After asking around, she found a room to rent. When the landlady handed Annette the key to an eight by ten foot apartment, she thanked her and tried not to cry. She couldn't risk bringing any more undue attention to herself. Once she was finally alone, however, Annette dropped her purse on the ground, bent to her knees and began to sob uncontrollably. She was free. She was really finally free.

Naa Akweley woke to find Afosua had already left for work and that she was all alone and idle. She hated being idle. This was not her home so she could not redecorate and, since she had fled her tormentor and husband, she had no one to cater to. But there was one person whom she had neglected in the last few weeks who still desperately needed her: her unborn baby.

Naa Akweley called her gynecologist's office and was able to get a last minute appointment. One of the benefits of being the wife of an influential man was that people went out of their way to make life comfortable for her. She laughed inwardly at the irony of it all. Her husband – to whom she owed this benefit – had done everything in his power to make her life anything but comfortable.

Naa Akweley left a note for Afosua and hired a taxi to drive her into Tema, where Silas Ofori's medical practice was. Ian had never been with her to an ob/gyn visit, and he had no clue where or how she received her prenatal care. His absence during the visit would not be out of the ordinary.

"Dr. Ofori will see you now," said the nurse cordially, soon after Naa Akweley was seated in the waiting room.

"How are you today?" asked Naa Akweley politely.

"I'm very fine, thank you," replied the nurse. "Please remove your clothes and put on this robe. He should be in momentarily."

Naa Akweley wondered if the nurse was this pleasant with all her patients. Ghanaian nurses had a reputation for being cruel and harsh, but that had never been her experience. She hoped that everyone received the same level of care; but then it dawned on her that this was a private practice and it was her money that was purchasing the professionalism. Naa Akweley decided that the nurse was insincere and prided herself on figuring out the other woman's character so quickly. Judging people was one of her strongest suits.

"Mrs. Blankson! I'm so happy to see you," said Dr. Ofori interrupting her thoughts.

"Hello, doctor. Yes, I know I've missed a few appointments."

"With your history of miscarriage, it is not a good thing that you do not see us regularly," he scolded.

Naa Akweley winced and nodded her head sheepishly. Her doctor had no idea what kind of hell she was facing at home.

"Let's begin your examination and see how everything is progressing," he said a little more kindly.

After measuring her belly and drilling her with several questions about her daily routine, he frowned.

"Your baby is measuring much smaller than he should," he said with concern. "How is your diet?"

"Fine, I suppose," she responded noncommittally.

"And what about alcohol consumption?"

"What do you mean?" she asked in sincere shock. How did he know?

"I'm sorry. I don't mean to offend you! I know your ministry's stand on consuming alcohol, but I have to weed out all the possibilities and at least ask," Dr. Ofori explained.

Naa Akweley hesitated before answering.

"No," she lied. "I have not been drinking. I don't drink."

The doctor misread her curt reply as indignation, when in fact she was actually frightened. What if she had harmed her baby?

"And what about stress?"

Naa Akweley replied cautiously. "What about it?"

"Well, I know that you probably spend a lot of your time doing charity work and praying for people, but that can take a toll on you at this stage," the doctor explained. "You are in your third trimester, and it's important to get rest if you can."

Naa Akweley nodded obediently, saying that she would begin to take more time for herself. She wished desperately that she could talk to her doctor honestly and tell him everything – about the abuse, about the drinking, about the bouts of depression she faced almost daily. But she was so ashamed and feared what the revelation might do to her reputation. She kept mum and got dressed.

"Thank you Dr. Ofori," she said as she left the examination room. "I will take all your advice into consideration."

"You're welcome," he smiled. "We'll look forward to the birth of a healthy baby boy in a few weeks, eh?"

Naa Akweley smiled in return and left for the waiting taxi outside. She would do all she could to keep her unborn baby healthy, but what about after he was born? Was she going to raise him alone or try to work things out with Ian? Would he grow up to resent her if he didn't have a father? The gravity of her future was more than she could bear for the moment. She abandoned thoughts of it and decided to focus on her present challenges. They were difficult enough.

******

Sophia stared stonily at the ceiling, waiting for her husband to climax so that he could get on a plane and go back to Nigeria. He usually showed up once a year to extort money from her, and his visits always ended with his penis inside her. It was not welcomed there.

John Ike's muscular buttocks lifted and dropped rhythmically as he dove deeper and deeper into Sophia. He thumbed her clitoris roughly, he sucked her nipples, bit her neck… anything to force her to respond to him. She refused to give in. John had so much power over her already, but in this area – the will to climax – she had total control and it bruised his ego to no end. John couldn't force her, no matter how hard he tried. He wanted complete dominance over Sophia, but like many Nigerian women she was not so easily handled. He gave up for the afternoon and pulled out of her, angrily cumming all over her trim thighs. Sophia looked down at her now wet legs and then back at the ceiling. Whatever emotions she was feeling, she did not betray them. She never gave her husband the satisfaction of evoking any sort of feeling. John stood up and put on his trousers. Sophia grabbed a towel and wiped herself before she spoke.

"Your money has been wired to your account," she said tersely. "It should hold you until next year."

"It should, but you never know."

"Look. That's over one million Naira! How can that not hold you?"

"Well, given that I harbored your smuggling and murderous father, I'd say that I decide how much is enough and for how long."

Sophia looked at John with utter contempt. How she had gotten entangled with him was beyond her understanding. She didn't even *like* men, at least not in that way. Somehow John had managed to convince her to marry him and carry on this charade that they had been playing for years. As John rightly said, her father was a smuggler and a wanted man, which was why she was estranged from him. She hadn't seen him since she was 16 and she had worked very hard to distance herself from any association with him. In Africa, your reputation is as valuable as any currency and Sophia's father's reputation threatened to ruin all that she had worked for. So when she discovered that John and her father had been working together for years in illegal trade, she was sick to her stomach. She cursed herself time and again for being so naïve. Now she was trapped in John's web of blackmail and deceit.

"It's not going to always be this way, John. I can promise you that," Sophia said with more bravery than she felt.

John stopped buttoning his shirt and strode over to where Sophia was standing. He grabbed her by the throat, cutting off her breath.

"If you ever breathe a word of my affairs, I can promise that you'll have more to worry about than the survival of your little seamstress shop," he said darkly.

Sophia glared at him defiantly, but soon relented and lowered her gaze. She knew what John was capable of.

"That's a good girl. Now go and bring me something to eat like a wife should. I have a flight to catch."

Sophia did as she was told and brought him a plate of food, watching him gobble it down like the swine that he was. She looked away and thought of Annette. She missed her so much.

*****

When Afosua got home, she found Naa Akweley perched in front of the television. Afosua felt awful about leaving her alone all day, but there was nothing she could do about it. Now she was leaving for Germany and Naa Akweley would be alone for even longer.

"Hi!" Naa said, unusually bright.

"How was your day?"

"Not bad. I went to the doctor and he suggested I get some R and R."

"I guess you're getting a lot of that here all alone. Sorry if I haven't been much company."

Naa Akweley shook her head.

"No. You have to work. You don't have time to entertain me."

Afosua felt relieved.

"Anyway, the doctor recommended that I take some time to myself," Naa continued. "I wondered if we might still make that trip to Dumbai? The one you told us about a few months ago?"

Afosua brightened immediately and then felt a wave of shame wash over her. It was time to confess her plan to her friend.

"Naa Akweley, I wasn't entirely honest with you. Yes, I wanted you to come to Dumbai with me because it is an amazing place, but the truth is I was planning on using you," she admitted. "I wanted to get access to your members and get them to buy in on a project I have in the village. I'm so sorry."

Naa Akweley turned off the television and eyed Afosua intently. Just two weeks ago she might have thrown a drink in Afosua's face following such an admission, but now she appreciated how brave Afosua was to be so forthcoming.

"I had a feeling," she conceded. "Many people try to use me to get to my husband or something in our ministry. I'm used to it. But I don't think that's the case with you anymore. Or am I wrong?"

"No. You're not wrong," said Afosua genuinely. "Besides, something much bigger has come up with work, so I may have to table the project or forgo it altogether."

"Great! Tell me about it over dinner. When do you leave?"

"In a week," said Afosua. "But I can still make arrangements for us to fly out there before I leave if you like. Did your doctor say it was okay?"

"He didn't say it wasn't," Naa Akweley mused. "Do you think Annette would still want to join us?"

"I don't know. I haven't seen or heard from her in days, which is odd. She's always good about calling me."

Naa Akweley nodded in agreement. Annette couldn't go a day without talking to someone. She always seemed to have her phone glued to her ear.

"I wonder what she's up to?"

"Let's try calling her in the morning. I'm sure she's okay."

****

Afosua and Naa Akweley pulled up to Hanger 3 at Kotoka International Airport at 10 am on Saturday morning. There wasn't a cloud in the sky, and Abdul Sayed promised that this was as good a day as any to fly.

"Did you have any luck reaching Annette?" asked Naa.

"No. Her phone just kept giving me an error message. It's very peculiar."

"Yes... it is. I'm sure she would have loved to join us on this trip. She seemed so keen on it before."

Afosua nodded, her broad rimmed sunglasses concealing her true feelings. She was worried. Should they cancel the trip to go look for Annette? Where would they begin?

"Are you ladies ready?" asked their pilot.

"Yes!" replied Naa Akweley brightly. "Let's get going!"

Abdul Sayed was a third generation Pakistani living in Ghana. He was tall, with wavy brown hair that lay just above his broad shoulders. His skin reminded Afosua of Caribbean beach sand, with little flecks of brown dotted all over. Locals called him *obroni* – a white man – but he was more Ghanaian than most... and certainly more fortunate than most. With his good looks and a sizeable inheritance, Abdul had started a small charter flight operation in the country carrying tourists to any destination they were willing to pay for. Phillips & Boakye often contracted his company to fly clients out to survey sites, but he had made it very clear to Afosua that he was personally available for private hire "anytime she wished." This was the first time she'd dared to take Abdul up on his offer.

"I'll be taking you in the turbo prop today." Abdul led them past a yellow amphibian helicopter. "It's a much more 'rustic' ride. You'll feel like you're on safari."

Afosua laughed.

"Living in Accra IS a safari," she countered. "It's a concrete jungle out here... or didn't you know?"

"True!" Abdul said, chuckling and taking the opportunity to touch her on the elbow.

When everyone was strapped in, he taxied onto the runway and took off. Naa Akweley felt her belly do flip flops and let out a gasp in surprise. Afosua noticed her reaction.

"Are you okay?"

"I'm fine!"

Naa Akweley was overcome by how beautiful her country looked from the air. She had flown plenty of times, but never once had she taken the opportunity to appreciate the gem that was her homeland. Within minutes they had flown beyond Accra and were heading northeast. Dumbai was in the Volta Region, and it would take them a little over an hour to arrive. Naa Akweley was sad that the flight was so short. She drank in the shimmering waters of Lake Volta and the expanse of unspoiled emerald green land. The view was a happy departure from the concrete jungle that she was so accustomed to.

The trio soon landed at Akpaka Airport, which was just large enough to avoid the label 'air strip.' The workers greeted them with enthusiasm and led them through a small terminal. Abdul ordered a beer at the chop bar once they were outside.

"You know it's odd, this is my second trip to Dumbai this week," he said through gulps of his lager. "I brought a group of Europeans up here about three days ago."

"Really?" asked Afosua. "Were they the usuals? Backpacks and Birkenstocks?"

Abdul shook his head.

"No. These were different. Suits and briefcases. Not the type that usually come up here looking to save souls or hunt antelope.

Afosua thoughtfully sipped on her Savannah Dry but soon excavated all thoughts of the strangers Abdul mentioned. She was entranced by the soft breeze filtering through the low-lying brush. A hush came over the table. No one wanted to force conversation in the face of such perfection.

"Madam, we have your car waiting for you," said a man in a brown uniform, interrupting the quiet.

"Thank you," said Afosua. She motioned for Naa Akweley to join her, who didn't hide her reluctance to do so. Afosua chuckled.

"Don't worry. It gets even better!"

They said their goodbyes to Abdul who said he'd be back on Sunday to pick them up.

"Just call if you need me," he said sweetly.

Afosua thanked him and promised she would.

The rented car took them to a three bedroom bungalow near the lake. It belonged to one of Afosua's many 'aunties' – not relatives by blood, but longtime acquaintances of her mother. Auntie Grace, a jovial woman with a pixie cut wig and lips pressed in perpetual smile, greeted them as they came through the gate.

"Ei! Afos! *Woezo*!" she shouted lifting her arms to embrace her guests. Unlike most Ghanaian women, Auntie Grace never refrained from displaying her affections in public. She kissed each of the women loudly on the cheek in welcome.

"Auntie, this is my friend Naa Akweley." Auntie Grace always put her in the best mood. "She's the one I told you would be joining me for the weekend."

The matriarch pulled Naa Akweley by the hand, never relaxing her grin.

"Then my dear you are most welcome!" she gushed. She glanced at Naa's protruding belly. "And you are pregnant! Come, let's go and feed the baby."

She ushered both of her guests into the house, instructing the house boy to bring their bags and put them in their rooms. As the three sauntered toward the back veranda, Afosua was reminded why Auntie Grace was always in such a pleasant mood. With spacious walkways and vibrant colors on every wall of the house, you couldn't help but be cheered by the atmosphere. Very few people knew it anymore, but Auntie Grace had built her dream home with money she had acquired as a go-go dancer in the 60s and 70s. She would travel to Akosombo and dance in the clubs for expatriates working on Nkrumah's dam. Her behavior was frowned upon by her peers in those days – male and female alike – who called her nothing but an "ashawo who got her money through sexy dancing," but she had been smart with her money, saved it and built a small empire. Underneath all Auntie Grace's exuberance, Afosua suspected that there might lay a hint of smugness. Afosua loved it; and she intentionally neglected to tell Naa Akweley about Auntie Grace's past. She didn't want her judging her.

Auntie Grace instructed Afosua and Naa Akweley to sit and called for the food to be brought out.

"I didn't know what you would take, so I have a bit of everything." She swept her hand over the heavy, wooden table.

Trays of grilled tilapia, banku, three kinds of savory stew and rice appeared.

"Auntie Grace, we can't eat all this," laughed Afosua.

"Yes you can. You are too thin, and we have to feed Naa's baby, isn't it?" admonished the older woman, pouring herself some wine. "And after we've rested, we can have a look at our project."

Naa Akweley nodded enthusiastically, unable to speak because her mouth was full of food. She had not eaten properly in days. Auntie Grace must have known Afosua well. All she had in her cupboards was rice and Cornflakes. For the first time in a long while, Naa Akweley felt like she was home.

*****

Annette had hardly left her new, rented room since she fled Mr. Prah's house. Late in the evening she went out to buy kenkey and fish and then sprinted back to her room to eat, hoping to remain unnoticed. She had to share a bathroom with the rest of the building, so she woke up at twilight before the rest of the tenants began stirring. Three days had gone by and she was beginning to settle into her new rhythm.

She picked up her towel and pail and tiptoed to the washroom. A voice in the pre-dawn darkness startled her.

"Ms. Annette?"

She stiffened and turned around, her eyes slowly adjusting to the dimness of the corridor.

"We've got her," said a deep male voice.

Suddenly two rough hands grabbed her from behind. Annette screamed in terror.

"Let me go! Let me go!" Annette cried as she was roughly pulled down the hall to a waiting car.

"What are you doing! Where are you taking me?"

"Annette Prah, you are under arrest," said a sinewy police officer as he shoved into the vehicle.

"Arrest?! Arrest for what?" she wailed incredulously.

"For theft… to the tune of ₵50,000."

Annette's heart threatened to stop beating. Damn that Mr. Prah. Damn him to hell. She stopped fighting and curled up helplessly in the corner of the police truck. There was no more fight left in her.

Auntie Grace called for her driver to come around to the front of the house.

"Samuel, we are going to the site," she informed him, as she settled into the back seat.

"Yes, madam," he responded mechanically. Samuel had been Auntie Grace's driver for over 15 years, and Afosua had never heard him say more than "yes madam" in that entire time. She thought the extreme cordiality between the driver and his employer was odd, given that they spent so much time together. Afosua concluded that Samuel had been privy to Auntie Grace's more clandestine destinations over the years and, wanting to keep his job and good standing, resorted to speaking as little as possible.

With each mile, Dumbai became more and more rural until the car reached an inlet on the river. Close to the banks was a small village of about six or eight mud and thatched huts. The huts were not uncommon in Ghana but what was special about them was the women who lived in them. Afosua, Naa Akweley and Auntie Grace got out of the car and walked into the center of the village.

"Mama, *woezo*!" said a robustly built woman to Auntie Grace. She shooed a few chickens away and instructed one of the young children milling around to bring some benches for ladies.

"Please, sit down," she instructed once the benches had been brought.

When everyone was seated, another group of ladies came out to greet the three visitors, shaking hands from right to left. After the customary pleasantries had been exchanged and everyone was assured that each other's family and homes were well, they got into the reason for the visit.

"I've brought Afosua so that you can tell her what decision has been made with the land," began Auntie Grace. "I understand we have very good news."

"Yes," said Auntie Aku, the woman who had greeted them initially. "We've consulted each other and decided that this will be a good project to undertake. We will lease you the land."

Afosua could scarcely contain her pleasure.

"This is wonderful news!" she gushed.

Unable to contain her curiosity, Naa Akweley finally asked what was going on.

"What project? What site? What are we doing here?"

One of the younger women brought a gourd and kalabash and offered a drink of water to Naa Akweley. She stiffened at the prospect of drinking village water, but Auntie Grace encouraged her to try it. Naa Akweley trusted the older woman, so she took a sip. Her eyes widened in surprise.

"It's so... sweet!"

"That's right," said Afosua emphatically. "There is a small tributary, not too far from here where the women fetch their water. They've done so for ages. This land is virgin and mostly untouched. I don't know what it is about the environment here, but the water has amazing properties."

Naa Akweley took another gulp of the cool, clear water. Her baby kicked in appreciation. She nodded her head. It was really good.

"What else do you notice about the women here?" asked Auntie Grace. "Look at them. Really look at them."

Naa Akweley looked around the small group, noticing them in earnest for the first time.

"Well, they all have very clear skin, for one thing. And they just seem... *healthy*, I guess."

Auntie Grace clapped in approval. "Exactly! These women are healthy. And we want to invite other women in Ghana to come here and get healthy too."

Afosua filled in the gaps. "The women have allowed us to lease the land and build a spa retreat. Don't you feel rejuvenated already?"

Naa Akweley had to admit that she did. There were no horns, no sirens, no street sellers squawking as they hawked their wares. There was only the soft rustling of leaves and this amazing water. There was peace.

"Can I see this tributary?"

Afosua grinned.

"I was hoping you would ask! Auntie, will you lead us there?"

******

Annette stood in the corner of the crowded holding cell that she shared with fifteen other women. She did not know where she was, but she gathered by the smell of sea water and rotting fish that she was somewhere near Osu, possibly James Town.

She fought the urge to break down and give in to complete despair. She had been crying since being captured earlier that morning. For the most part, her cell mates left her alone. When a stocky brown skinned woman had tried to bully her earlier, Annette had reached out and clawed her in the face. There would have been a fight if one of the guards had not intervened. Each of the other women seemed too wrapped up in their own misery to try to engage anyone else beyond sucking their teeth or to sullenly order another inmate to get out of her way.

Annette's thoughts on her miserable situation were interrupted when a guard barked at her.

"Heh! You there! Ehhh, you the thief! You have a visitor."

Annette did not turn around until she heard a familiar croak.

"Hello darling."

Mr. Prah's smug face was staring at her through the rusty black bars. She greeted him with a stony stare.

"So you thought you were going to leave me just like that eh?" he chuckled to himself. "If it were that easy, I'm surprised you didn't try to get away earlier."

"I didn't steal that money, Mr. Prah. It's mine."

"Ah. If I say you stole it, then you stole it, my dear," he countered. "You have no job. You have no income. How did you come by the money? It doesn't matter if it was in your room. The money was in MY house. Of course you stole it from me!"

He lowered his voice and moved in closer.

"Who would believe otherwise?"

Annette knew he was right. And even if there was doubt about her guilt, Mr. Prah had enough money to pay to make it go away.

"Why are you doing this?" she whimpered. "Why can't you just let me have peace?"

"Because you owe me," Mr. Prah said simply, as though the question surprised him.

"I don't owe you anything!" Annette raged. "My marrying you was to resolve my father's debt. Don't you think twenty years of my life and my youth are payment enough?"

Mr. Prah snickered.

"It's enough when I say it's enough. But I'll make you a deal. You promise never to try to leave again, and you can come out of here now. All you have to do is live up to your vows from our wedding day. You owe me your undying devotion and fealty."

Annette laughed. It was a hollow, dark sound.

"It's funny you should use that word – fealty. Because that's exactly what I've been for two decades: a servant in your fiefdom."

She shook her head.

"No more, Mr. Prah. No more! I'd rather die than come back to you."

Kwame Prah clicked his tongue disapprovingly.

"Oh, Annette. You poor, stupid slut. Look around you and think about it! You have no one on your side, and you are nobody unless I say so."

He turned to leave the cell, pausing to speak once more.

"They won't hang you or shoot you, of course," he mused. "It's a shame, but Ghana has come a long way since the days of the firing squad, lucky for you. ₵50,000 is a huge sum of money, no matter how you slice it. At best they'll keep you here until the judge says the debt has been paid off. But the better offer is to confess and come home with me."

He held out his gnarly hand as if beckoning her. Annette took three steps back in revulsion.

"Very well."

Mr. Prah called for the guard and ambled out of the police station. When she could no longer hear his footsteps, Annette crumpled to the floor and gasped for air. It was the first time she had ever stood up to Mr. Prah. It left her breathless.

******

Afosua pulled out a notebook and scribbled her ideas for the wellness spa for Naa Akweley to see.

"This room will be for meditation."

"Or prayer," countered Naa Akweley. "You don't want to put people off by saying 'meditation.'"

"Fine, meditation and SILENT prayer. And we're going to send young women from the area into Accra to get training in massage therapy and wellness. I think it will be good all around."

Naa Akweley looked at Afosua, who was glowing for the first time since she'd met her. Knowing the tragedy that Afosua had suffered through not so long ago, Naa admired her for putting her energies into something so positive. Perhaps she could learn from her. Perhaps she could be this happy, too.

"Afosua, I'd like to partner with you, if you'd let me," Naa Akweley said timidly. "I know this is your project and all..."

"I was hoping you'd want to. I know it would be good for you... for us. I could use your influence to get this off the ground. People respect you."

Naa Akweley smiled wryly. *Too bad my husband didn't respect me...*

Auntie Grace interrupted their conversation.

"Who are those people over there?" she said, pointing across the river bank.

Afosua squinted to look.

"Those must be the white people Abdul was talking about."

"Eh. I see," mulled Auntie Grace. "Let's go pay them a visit, shall we?"

"Oh Auntie, we can't just go over there and –"

"Don't be silly. Of course we can. See? The boy has already brought a canoe over. Get in."

Naa Akweley opted to stay on the other side. Afosua promised that they would be back soon. She was only going to indulge Auntie Grace's curiosity. When the canoe approached, Afosua recognized a male figure among the group.

"Mr. Boakye?"

The mention of his name turned caused Harold Boakye to do an about face and put him nose to nose with Afosua.

"Ms. Gyemfi," he said coldly. "What are you doing here?"

"I might ask you the same question… sir."

"I would assume that you would be preparing for your trip to Germany. Instead I find you here gallivanting on the waters' edge with villagers."

Afosua touched Auntie Grace's arm to keep her from retorting. This was still her boss, no matter how rude he was. A tall blond haired man inserted himself into their conversation.

"Do you know this young lady?" he asked Harold Boakye.

"Yes. I'm Afosua Gyemfi," she said, holding out her hand to shake his. "I'm a senior actuary for Phillips & Boakye."

The blond smiled.

"Oh wonderful! Jurgen Gunnarson." He pumped Afosua's hand enthusiastically.

The name sounded so familiar. Then it hit her: Gunnarson; from the Swedish account. But the site for Swedish account wasn't anywhere near Dumbai...

Afosua heart skipped a beat. What was Mr. Boakye up to?

Mr. Boakye's eyes bore into Afosua's. Whatever her thoughts were, she kept them guarded. He was unable to read them.

"Well Mr. Gunnarson, it has been very nice meeting you under such pleasant conditions. But as Mr. Boakye said, I should be getting back to Accra and preparing for my business trip."

Jurgen's pale blue eyes traveled the expanse of her body. Afosua became uncomfortably aware that the cool wind was coaxing her nipples, which were now wantonly straining against the thin cotton shirt she was wearing. The Swede didn't even bother trying to hide that he was ogling her.

"Then I'll see you again soon! I'll be in Accra with Mr. Boakye in a few days myself."

Harold Boakye nodded silently in affirmation.

"Right. Auntie, shall we?"

Afosua grabbed the older woman's hand and ordered the boy to row back to the other end of the shore.

"What was that all about?" asked Auntie Grace.

Afosua's eyes blazed with determination. "I don't know, but I'm going to find out."

Gertrude sat at her dining room table admiring her newly procured passport. She cradled it in her hands so that it would not make contact with the linoleum table cloth, as though the floral plastic might sully it. She was giddy with the thought of leaving the country for the first time.

Her mother brought her a plate of food. The grilled chicken breast she'd prepared was cut into slender rectangles and lay delicately on top of piping hot jollof rice. Gertrude's mother sat opposite her, watching her daughter eat with admiration.

"I'm so proud of you, *davi*. I never dreamed that my child would grow up to be so important."

"I'm just a secretary, Ma," Gertrude said sullenly.

Her mother rebuked her gently.

"Never say that. You are much more than that. You hear?"

"Yes, Ma."

Gertrude wanted to broach the subject of her father. This seemed the perfect time. Her mother always got so defensive when she brought him up, but surely now she would understand?

"Ma," she began shakily, "I'm going to Germany... as you know... so maybe don't you think we should talk about my father?"

Cecelia chuckled under her breath.

"Ho. Why? Do you think you will go and meet him there?"

Gertrude shook her head defensively. "No... of course not."

"Then why should we talk about him because you are going to Germany?"

"No reason, Ma," said Gertrude, abandoning the conversation altogether. "I'm going to go and read over our files now. Thank you for lunch."

Cecelia watched her daughter, now a young professional, walk despondently to the bedroom that they shared in a cramped efficiency house. There were no secrets between them, except this one. She could have spared Gertrude's feelings by telling her everything about her father, but that would mean exposing her own; she had never been brave enough to face them.

******

Abdul was waiting at the airport to pick up Afosua and Naa Akewley as promised, which was good. Afosua was eager to get back to Accra so that she could get to the bottom of the mystery. She was so preoccupied by Mr. Boakye's presence in Dumbai that she barely heard a word Naa Akewley was saying during the flight.

"Afosua, did you catch that?"

"Heh?"

"I asked you if you've done a cost estimate for building on the site," repeated Naa Akweley. "I think we should get as much on paper as early as possible. I want to get as much finished as I can before the baby comes."

Afosua watched Naa Akweley rub her belly lovingly. She was pleased that the woman had found a new focus other than her misery. She wanted to share her exuberance, but she couldn't concentrate on the health spa right now.

"I have done some preliminary work but I'll get you something more substantial when I get back from Germany."

Naa Akweley smiled and nodded. She spoke, suddenly remembering something.

"What happened when you went to see those people on the other side of the river bank yesterday?"

Afosua furrowed her forehead.

"My boss was there."

"Really? He has business in Dumbai?"

"I don't know. I have to tread carefully with this until I have all my facts. It's probably better if I don't speak about it until I know anything for sure."

Naa Akweley nodded and turned her attention to the ground beneath them. They would be landing back in Accra in a few minutes, and she wanted to enjoy what remained of the view for as long as she could. She reveled in the hope of her new future and said a silent prayer of thanks to God for it.

Back at Kotoka, Abdul had already arranged for a car to take the women to Afosua's house.

"I hope to see you again soon?" he said, reaching out to shake Afosua's hand gently.

Afosua wondered how he could manage to be so professional and utterly seductive at the same time. She smiled up at him and promised that they would need his business soon and often. He smiled with self-satisfaction when the two ladies had driven off.

Now that they were on the ground, Afosua was finally able to check her cell phone for messages. There was a text from an unknown number.

Annette has been arrested. Plz call back

"Oh my God!"

"What? What is it?" asked Naa Akweley

"It's Annette. She's been arrested!"

"That poor girl," said Naa Akweley somberly. "She'll definitely need our prayers."

Afosua bristled. This could not be left to mere prayer alone.

"They hell you say! She needs a lawyer. And I know just the one. I'm sure Mr. Prah is behind this, that old warty bastard."

******

Annette was beginning to feel ill. She had only been in jail for two days, and she felt certain she wasn't going to survive much longer there. The police station did not feed prisoners, so Annette should have been grateful for the morsel of moldy bread that one of her cellmates was kind enough to share with her. She could barely bring herself to bite into it, though. The conditions were beyond unsanitary, and she refused to bathe outside under the watchful and lascivious eyes of the guards. She was dirty, hungry and miserable. But she was not completely broken just yet. She stared at a slate grey wall and fixed her eyes on a set of claw marks etched into its flat surface. Someone had gone mad in here and tried to scratch their way out. Would she be driven to that point?

"Heh! You! The half-caste thief. You have a visitor."

Annette rolled her eyes and prepared to face off with Mr. Prah again. She felt a surge of bile rise up in her throat as she whipped around. Suddenly, the world stopped.

"Hello Annette."

"Sophia? What are you doing here?"

Sophia rushed over to hug her through the rusty jail bars. Annette leaned against them, weeping with relief.

"No touching the prisoners!" the guard barked, forcing the two women to back away.

"How did you know I was here?"

"It's all over the news," replied Sophia. "You've been accused of embezzling from Mr. Prah."

"Then what little reputation I have is obliterated," mourned Annette. Then she chuckled sardonically. "Nothing sells more newspapers than a detested socialite locked up in a local prison, does it?"

Sophia was at a loss for words. It hardly seemed the time to try to make a joke.

"I brought you something to eat." Sophia passed the food to the guard to inspect it. After he fished out a huge cube of beef and smacked greedily at it, he passed it back to Annette who devoured it with gratitude.

"Have you come to bail me out too?"

Sophia shook her head.

"I asked, and they said you had a bail hearing set for Monday when the courts reopen. Has anyone said anything to you?"

"No," whispered Annette. "I don't have a lawyer, and I have been falsely accused. I – I don't know what to do."

"We'll figure it out."

"Time's up!" ordered the guard. "You have to go!"

"My friend you don't have to be so rude, eh?" snapped Sophia.

Sophia's angry Nigerian accent seemed to make the guard back down, but only slightly. He stepped in to usher her out. Annette reached her hand through the jail bars.

"Wait! Sophia… what you said the last time I saw you… was it…"

Sophia reached back and gripped her hand.

"None of it was true," she assured her. "None of it."

"Let's go!" said the guard impatiently.

"Look here, *jo*, if you continue to speak to me this way I will have you fired!" growled Sophia.

Annette strained to hear the fading sounds of Sophia's thunderous hail of rebukes and insults as she left the premises. She sank to the ground and allowed tears of relief to wash her face. Sophia loved her and, in that moment, it was all Annette cared about.

****

The phone rang early on Monday morning, snapping Afosua into reality.

"Afosua?"

"Yes?"

"This is Sophia Ike."

"The designer?"

"Yes."

Why was Sophia Ike calling her so early on a week day? How had she gotten her number?

"Annette and I are… good friends," explained Sophia. "She's mentioned you to me on several occasions. I sent you a text message yesterday to tell you about her arrest."

"Yes!" said Afosua excitedly. "Yes, I got it. I was too overwhelmed to give you a call back… I'm sorry."

It had all seemed like a bad dream the day before. Now Afosua had to face the fact that her friend was in real danger.

"I figured that the two of you were close," continued Sophia. "Have you seen the news?"

"Only that she is being accused of embezzlement, which is absurd, because Annette has no dealings with any of Prah's enterprises at all."

"It doesn't matter. The sad thing is that around here you can be accused and jailed without proof, if the person accusing you has enough money to purchase your guilt."

The enormity of the situation had not escaped Afosua.

"Sophia, I've got a call I need to make. I promise I'll call you back when I have more details."

The two women hung up and Afosua got out of bed to shower. There was only one woman who could help Annette now, and she owed Afosua a favor.

"Naa Akweley, I'm leaving to see that barrister I was telling you about. I shouldn't be gone long."

Naa Akweley rolled over to wave good bye, her round belly making every movement slow and deliberate.

"Call me with any details if you can please."

"Of course," replied Afosua.

As Afosua walked by the mirror, she noticed her hair was unkempt. She didn't have time to style it.

"Can I borrow your hair clip to pull my hair back?"

Naa Akweley pulled the clip out of her ponytail and handed it to Afosua, then rolled back over and pretended to go back to sleep. She was worried for Annette but she didn't want to discuss her anxiety with Afosua. She felt the need to portray confidence in order to mask the helplessness she felt.

Sometime later, Afosua navigated her car into a parking space in front of the offices of Lydia Oppong, Esq. and waited. Lydia wasn't the most abhorred barrister in Ghana, but she was certainly one of the most successful. Usually the two exist in tandem. Lydia was the first woman to bring down an MP, forcing him to resign amid a scandal that shocked the nation. When the minister for education in 1977 had seduced and impregnated her, then a young law student, he refused to acknowledge paternity of the baby and embarked on a campaign to bring Lydia to disrepute. He alleged that she was part of syndicate extorting money from 'big men' by falsely accusing them of indecent acts. What he hadn't banked on was Lydia's meticulous note taking and inquisitive nature. When the minister invited her to his offices for evening romps, the young woman riffled through his files when he wasn't paying attention and found records to prove he was siphoning official funds and diverting them for personal use – which included the purchase of an impressive porn collection. This was not to be borne in such a Christian country! When the MP was forced into court to face charges and found guilty for his illegal activity, a 22 year old Lydia stood on the steps of the courthouse and famously declared:

"He thought I was some *fiyanga* girl he could just mess over. But the system has taught the education minister a thing or two today!"

Lydia Oppong continued to pursue her law degree and had her baby; but she saw that the law was made more powerful when a picture told the stories that words couldn't. She became a divorce lawyer and, over the years, hired a select group of secondary school girls to tail husbands suspected of cheating. Armed with embarrassing images of men in compromising positions in seedy parts of town, divorces were usually granted quickly to Lydia's clients to spare public embarrassment. For this, she was despised by men. Afosua was one of the young girls who had worked for Lydia.

Unlike the others, she had refused money for her wages. Instead, she asked that Ms. Oppong represent her in trial if she ever needed it.

A woman knocked on her car window as Afosua waited.

"Can I help you?" asked a stocky girl with plump, frosted lips. "This is private parking space."

"I'm waiting for Barrister Oppong," said Afosua tersely.

"Do you have an appointment?"

"No…"

"Well she won't see you without an appointment," said the girl matter-of-factly. "I'm her personal assistant."

"Good for you!" Afosua shot back. "Now if you'll excuse me, you're letting all my A/C out."

Waving her hand dismissively, Afosua rolled up the window and turned her attention away from the shocked young woman, who stalked into the office in a huff. Five minutes later, a shiny black Mercedes with tinted windows pulled in beside her. Afosua smiled to herself. The car was very much like her former boss: all show on the outside, concealing something within. She got out to greet the woman. If Lydia was surprised to see Afosua, she didn't show it.

"I suppose you're here to collect on what I owe you?" said the older woman, taking her by the hand.

"Yes, madam," Afosua said, allowing herself to be led into the office.

"Let's hear it then. It's been ten years since I've seen you, so it must be something big!"

Lydia turned to the plump assistant.

"Bring us a tray with tea please, Millicent, and see that we are not disturbed for a while."

Afosua shot Millicent a triumphant glare before ducking into the office.

"Now tell me everything my dear," said Lydia, leaning back in her chair.

Afosua launched into the details as she knew them. To her surprise, Lydia was already well abreast of the issue.

"Of course it's nonsense," she scoffed. "But we're dealing with public opinion and a lot of money. Women like Annette – beautiful, aloof and privileged – are hated and admired by our people, by all people, for that matter. If Mr. Prah can make the case that she was greedy and show a pattern of greed, he might have a shot. I don't know what kind of proof he's got, but he must be feeling very confident to have gone as far as to have her arrested."

"Or just malicious."

"That too."

"So will you do it?"

Lydia was aghast.

"You are asking me to bring down one of the titans of Ghanaian industry. A man with a history longer than the river he's named after, spent making shady deals that screw the little guys and take advantage of their poverty. How can you even ask, Afosua? Of course I will!"

Afosua almost leapt out of her chair to smother Lydia with a hug, but composed herself and stuck out her hand.

"Then we'll be in touch. I leave for Europe in a few days for work. I'll help anyway I can before then."

"Millicent will see you out. I'll work on getting Annette out of jail this afternoon. I can get her fast-tracked for a bail hearing. Leave it to me."

Afosua saw herself out and skipped down to her car. Her heart was soaring. Then her stomach began to grumble. She had completely forgotten to eat that morning. She made sure her car was locked and walked over to A&C Mall to pick up a pastry. As she entered the bakery, Ian Blankson nearly ran over her on his way out. She drew a sharp breath.

"You… Don't I know you?"

The corners of his mouth curved slightly upward in foggy recollection.

"Yes," replied Afosua stiffly. "We've met before."

"Ahhh… yes! At my church. You were looking for my accountant. Did you ever find what you were looking for?" The man was smooth. He was inching his body closer to hers. Had he no shame? His wife had been missing for over a week and he didn't seem to have noticed.

"Everything turned out fine, thank you. Have a good day, *Pastor.*"

Afosua slid past him and walked up to the counter to make her order. As she glanced at her reflection in the mirror behind the counter, she noticed that Ian was still standing there, staring at her backside. He was such a pig! By the time she'd paid for her donuts and turned around, he was gone.

Good riddance.

Lydia Oppong went to the trunk of her car and pulled out a simple batik dress and a pair of flip-flops and stuffed them into a plastic bag. She strode confidently into the police station and approached the warden's desk.

"I'm here to see my client, Annette Prah." Her addressee was a sleepy man in a dark blue uniform. "Can you lead me to her?"

The warden looked Lydia up and down slowly before speaking. He motioned at a lurking lieutenant near the exit door.

"Aboagye!"

"Yessah!"

"Bring the half-caste girl. Her lawyer is here."

"Yessah!"

Lydia sauntered over to a wooden bench and sat, not waiting to be offered a seat. She was the type of woman who had learned to make herself comfortable no matter the surroundings. When Annette finally emerged from the dark corridor, it seemed to take her a while to adjust to the light. The holding cells had been built during the colonial era with the aim of breaking the human spirit. They had little light and even less fresh air.

Lydia rose to shake Annette's hand, who took hers gingerly.

"Mrs. Prah, Lydia Oppong. I've been retained to represent you."

"I'm so glad," breathed Annette with relief. "What happens now?"

"Now my dear, we leave for court. You have a bail hearing. We won't be returning to these quaint accommodations any time soon, I assure you of that."

There was only one vehicle assigned to the station and it was out on patrol. When it had been agreed that the lieutenant would join them in Lydia's car to ensure that Annette would not try to abscond, they set off for the high court in Accra Central. Annette sat in the back seat and changed out of her filthy clothes. She slipped the dress that Lydia brought for her over her head and put on the slippers.

"There is a face towel under the seat," said Lydia. "Wipe your face as best you can. We want the judge to make as much eye contact with you as possible. No one wants to look at a woman with a dirty face."

*****

Afosua went home and pulled out her laptop. There was no point in going into the office since she was already late. Besides, she wanted to avoid Mr. Boakye for as long as possible. He still didn't know that she had saved the forbidden files on her thumb drive weeks ago. She fished the small device out of a drawer where she kept her DVDs and plugged it in.

She tabbed through the prospectus for the Swedish account until she found the organization chart. She recognized Jurgen's name and title, and deduced that the two other names were the men she saw on the riverbank in Dumbai. The forth name just seemed weird... almost like it was made up. Lark H. O'Keyoab, CFO.

"O'Keyoab" was not a Scandinavian name. Who was this character managing their money? Was he Irish? Scottish? Neither group traditionally had much business in Ghana. Afosua scrolled through the files until she got to the financials. Whoever Lark was, he was smart enough to spread the assets around several banks in the country. She stared at the name long and hard.

Lark H. O'Keyoab...

Loyed Harkboa...

Harold Boakye

"Oh my God!" whispered Afosua.

"What is it?" asked Naa Akweley, who was now looking over her shoulder. "Is that our prospectus for Dumbai?"

"Huh? Oh no, no. It's just something for work. Confidential." Afosua closed the laptop quickly.

She got up and pulled out the binder that had all the details for Dumbai and handed it to Naa Akweley, a tornado of anxiety swirling in her chest. How much had Naa Akweley seen?

"Why don't you take a look over it and tell me what you think it's missing? I'm sure it could use another critical eye."

Naa Akweley brightened. It was the first time in a while that someone had asked her input on a proposal... other than where the next all-night prayer meeting should be held or if all the ladies should wear power blue or white for Founder's Day Sunday. She clutched the binder close to her chest.

"I'll have feedback for you tonight."

"Great. I have to dash out for a minute." Afosua grabbed her keys. "Can I get you anything?"

She was nervous and trying hard to act normal. If Naa Akweley caught on that something was wrong, she didn't let it show.

"No, I'm fine. I'll see you when you get back."

Afosua was already closing the door when Naa finished her response. Naa turned back to the laptop on the table and opened the lid. The screen was blank and password protected. It was just as well. She felt a sudden sense of guilt for trying to snoop into her friend's work affairs and reclosed the lid. She went back into the bedroom to dutifully pour over the paperwork for their new project.

******

Annette stood at the defense table, feeling exposed and frightened. Lydia Oppong was now cloaked in a black robe and under a yellowing wig that barely covered her thick, permed hair. Annette envied Lydia her shroud. She wished that she could borrow it to cloak herself, if only for a moment.

The judge presiding over her bond hearing was an elderly man, about sixty or more. His tired eyes were vacant and watery, probably from years spent reading dull case law late into the night. A court secretary handed him a copy of Annette's speedily drawn up motion, which he read with impassiveness. Finally he waved for Lydia Oppong to approach the bench.

"Where is council for Mr. Prah?" he asked irritably.

"M'Lord, I am uncertain why Mr. Prah's attorney or Mr. Prah himself is not here for that matter," replied Lydia, putting emphasis on her next words. "However my client and I are here... as we have the *highest* regard for the court's time."

"Well your client was arrested for theft, so I doubt she had anywhere else to be," quipped the judge.

Lydia waited silently for the judge's orders. There was no point in getting on his bad side by being combative. He waved her back to the defense table to stand by Annette before addressing her directly.

"Mrs. Prah, how do you plead to the charges as they have been leveled against you?"

"Not guilty, my lord," Annette said in a clear strong voice, just as Lydia had instructed her to do.

The magistrate sat up in his chair. He was so accustomed to criminals coming into his court room weeping and blaming 'Satan for casting a spell on them.' This display of confidence was a departure from the norm. His watery eyes examined Annette from crown to sole with either longing or pity – it was hard to tell. A ray of sunlight caught a bit of her curly brown hair, casting an angelic glow about her. The judge softened a little.

"Very well. We shall set bail at ₵6,000. You will be remanded into the custody of your lawyer and will return to court in three weeks for trial."

"Thank you, M'lord," said Lydia.

She tapped Annette on the shoulder and led her out of the dingy courtroom. Annette was stunned.

"Wait. What – that's it?" she asked feverishly. "It was all so sudden!"

Lydia chuckled.

"My dear, what you will find is that in our society, appearance is everything. It looks very bad that neither Mr. Prah nor his lawyer showed up, and it would look even worse for the judge to throw you back into a cell when the party accusing you was not present to object or to present evidence against you. Ultimately, the law plays itself out as how justice *ought* to look."

Annette did not understand this at all, but she was grateful. After Lydia provided the bail and filed her receipts, she ushered Annette to the car.

"So where can I drop you off at? Your parents'? A relative's maybe?"

Annette shook her head.

"Mr. Prah isolated me from my family years ago. I have no one…" Her thoughts turned to Sophia, but that was too fanciful a dream.

Lydia tapped on her temple and sighed, as though she were waging a violent internal war. She was not in the practice of harboring strays, but she did owe Afosua this favor and would see it through.

"I have a spare room at my house," she offered begrudgingly. "You can stay with me until we sort something else out."

Annette looked down at her lap and closed her eyes. She imagined that she was already lying in a real bed, with real sheets… Within moments she was fast asleep. Had she been awake, she would have seen a man in a suit kicking his back left tire on the side of the road. Some stupid *kubolor* boy had left his stack of wood and nails behind his car and now his tire was flat. Lydia chuckled as she drove by and watched the enraged man frantically try and call a mechanic to fix the tire. Now he was late for court! Mr. Prah's lawyer really ought to have been more careful where he parked.

Tony tapped his foot on the restaurant floor until Afosua arrived. She had sounded so intense on the phone, more agitated than normal. He was looking forward to seeing her but wondered what could possibly have set her on edge so badly. Perhaps she was having regrets about the last time they were together.

A few moments later Afosua walked into the door and hurried to his table. He stood and pulled out a chair for her, unsure if he should hug her or shake her hand. Her skin was dewy and she looked flushed. Was she feverish? He sat in the chair next to hers and protectively took her hands into his.

"Are you alright?" he asked with sincere concern.

Afosua waved the waiter over and asked for water.

"I'm fine," she lied.

When the water arrived she took a deep gulp. When her heart rate was a bit steadier, she began to dig around in her purse and pulled out the thumb drive that contained the details on Jurgen's account. She placed it in Tony's hand.

"What's this?"

"It's something I need you to hold on to while I'm gone," she whispered, leaning in closer to Tony. He was instantly distracted by the light scent of her perfume and her quickened breath.

"You mustn't let anyone see this under any circumstances, okay?"

The urgency in her voice brought him back to focus.

"What's on it?" he asked anxiously. "Why is it such a secret?"

Afosua scooted her chair closer to his and forced his gaze to meet hers directly. She was about to speak when she noticed that the other patrons were staring at them suspiciously.

"Let's get out of here. I'll tell you everything."

****

Lydia Oppong's house was colossal. Centered in the cobblestone court yard was a massive fountain, fashioned to depict an African woman pouring water back into a river. Twin doors made of mahogany and copper overlay beckoned visitors to the entrance. Each door was carved with a pictorial narrative, compelling one to pause and consider its mute tale. Annette would have spent more time trying to decipher the carvings had Lydia not shooed her into the house.

"Come and I'll show you your room."

Lydia led Annette through a small maze of rooms, pointing out the kitchen, three living rooms and back yard.

"If you swim, there is a pool," she said noncommittally. "I don't keep spare swimming suits, but I'm sure we can find one in town."

Annette nodded in acknowledgement. She had never learned to swim, but would love to dip her feet into the water. The two women ascended the helical stair case and passed by Lydia's home office and several other rooms. Finally, at the far end of the corridor they came to the guest suite. It was painted mint green and there was a crisp white comforter on the bed. It was clean, but uninviting – as though it was decorated to encourage brief stays.

"I hope it will suit you?" said Lydia.

"Yes! Of course," replied Annette. "It's lovely – simple, but elegant."

Lydia pointed to the right side of the room.

"You'll find a bathroom here through those doors. It's all yours, of course. I'll see to it that the girl brings you some soap and fresh towels."

"Thank you."

The lawyer looked down at her watch and excused herself. She had to get back to her office and see to another case.

"When I get back we will begin to discuss our strategy in detail," she informed Annette. "There's a lot of research we have to do if we're to deal with Kwame Prah."

Annette nodded solemnly. Even the sound of his name struck terror in her. If he could find her in Asylum Down, how much easier would it be for him to find her in this grand place? Lydia read Annette's concern immediately. She put her hand on her shoulder and squeezed it gently.

"No one is going to force you from here," she assured her. "For one, they would be trespassing, and for another, you are free on bond. Unless you reoffend within the space of the next few weeks, no one has reason to come looking for you."

"But I didn't commit an offence in the first place," Annette pointed out.

"And that is our task to prove in court," replied Lydia. "I'll see you tonight when I get back from the office. Call Josephine if you need anything."

Annette took off her flip flops and heard the grand wooden doors downstairs swing shut a few minutes later. She turned on the hot water in the shower until the room was steamy and let it scald her skin. The combined weight of the flowing liquid and her newfound relief forced her to the shower floor, where she lay until the temperature turned frigid and finally forced her to bed.

*****

Afosua followed Tony to the door of his home. The gardener cast the two of them a knowing glance but continued to cut the leafy bushes that surrounded the inside of Tony's compound. Tony shouted a greeting at him.

"Kofi, how be?"

"Oh fine boss!" Kofi chortled. He gave Afosua a wide smile. She gave him a courtesy nod in return.

"Will you have something? Some water, or a drink perhaps?"

"No, thanks," said Afosua, settling into the closest chair.

Tony poured himself some orange juice and sat next to her. He waited until she was ready to speak.

"I think someone at Phillips & Boakye is engaging in something fraudulent."

Tony's eyes widened.

"Who do you suspect? And of what?"

"I'd rather not say who, and I can't tell you of what until I have all my facts in order," she said evasively. "I just need someone I can trust right now – and the only person I kind of trust is you."

"Only kind of?" he murmured softly, taking her hand. "Afosua, I hope you know that I would never hurt you... and if there is any way I can help you, I will. How can I help you?"

She smiled and covered his other hand with hers.

"Just keep this hidden and safe till I get back from my business trip. I leave on Thursday, but I'll be back a week from then."

Tony nodded.

"No problem."

Their shared moment of faith sent a surge through their clasped hands. Tony reached to Afosua and brushed her cheek softly. He then kissed her passionately and deeply, cupping her face with both his hands. Feeling herself surrender to desire Afosua moaned but suddenly pushed him away and stood up. Alarmed, Tony flew to his feet as well. What had he done wrong?

"Which way is your bedroom?" Afosua asked, reaching out to unbutton his shirt, pausing only to look at him expectedly.

Tony smiled and quickly led her away, praying with every step that next week would come and go quickly.

Thursday came far faster than Gertrude had counted on. She tried to quell her apprehension as the flight to Frankfurt was called. She and Afosua had spent the last three days poring over strategy, but she still felt nervous and unprepared. She prayed that she wouldn't sabotage the venture with her inexperience. Her mother had come to see her off and waved goodbye with tears in her eyes. The two of them had never been apart. Gertrude had never been to boarding school, never had her own apartment, and never been away from home. Her mother was extremely proud of her and would miss her terribly.

Unfamiliar with customs procedures, Gertrude followed Afosua's lead. She placed her suitcases on the conveyor belt in the same manner as Afosua and, when they got on the plane, ordered everything Afosua did. Her mimicry did not go unnoticed. When they were safely airborne Afosua tapped Gertrude on the hand.

"You need to have more confidence in yourself, Gertrude. Mark chose you for this job because he saw something in you that made him believe you would be successful. Don't prove him wrong by doubting yourself."

Gertrude nodded in concession. She had to get a grip on herself, and now. If she kept thinking about messing up, she eventually would. She closed her eyes and daydreamed of a triumphant return to her own corner office at Phillips & Boakye. Wasn't that the point of all her hard work? Soon she drifted off to sleep. When Gertrude awoke, a stewardess was bringing her an immigration form and a hot towel to wipe her face. As the tires of the plane hit the runway, Gertrude's heart leapt with sudden a realization: she was on German soil, connecting with a part of her heritage that she had previously only studied but never experienced. She instantly felt stronger.

A representative from Deutsch Tech Labs met Afosua and Gertrude at the arrival hall. He was a wiry man with thin grey hair and an even thinner smile. He seemed unapproachable and disagreeable, hardly the sort of person one sends to welcome two visitors from abroad. When he had confirmed that the two women were from Phillips & Boakye, he led them to a waiting vehicle outside. Afosua steadied herself for a drive filled with icy silence with this man and settled into her seat with her arms crossed. Gertrude was more wont to converse, however.

"Wie ist das Wetter in Deutschland zu dieser Zeit?" she asked, inquiring after the weather.

The driver seemed taken aback by her fluency.

"Sprechen Sie Deutsch?" he asked in surprise.

"Ja," Gertrude replied smilingly. "Mein Name ist Gertrude."

"Klause," said the man, looking at Gertrude in the review mirror. He seemed to like what he saw a lot better, now that he was studying her.

The two carried on a lengthy conversation for the next fifteen minutes, discussing pleasantries like football and fashion. It seemed lively, and Afosua was glad that Gertrude was making such a positive impression early on. This freed her to contemplate what she was going to do about Harold Boakye when she got back to Accra.

Klaus shuttled the guests to The Pure Hotel and helped get their bags to their rooms. Afosua assured him that the bellhop could manage, but it was clear that he wanted to hang around Gertrude for as long as possible. She didn't blame him. Gertrude was very pretty, after all.

An itinerary was placed on the night stands in each of their rooms. After the women had rested, they were to meet the team assigned to the *asaa* project for dinner. The next day they were to leave for Dresden to visit the lab and remain there for the rest of the week.

Gertrude was disappointed that they would be leaving the hotel. Every room was bathed in white. It was clean... and *pure*, just as the name of the facility said. She looked out of the window to take in the new sights. In a way, it wasn't that different from Accra. People milled about in the street, looking very busy. They just didn't seem to have as much urgency in their steps as Ghanaians.

"I'm going to take a shower and a nap before dinner," said Afosua, snapping her out of her thoughts. "I think you ought to do the same. We can go over our notes just before we go down."

Gertrude nodded in agreement and turned to get her suitcase.

"Good job today by the way," Afosua added before leaving. "That was very impressive. I think a touch of informality is going to help us win this bid. But just a touch, okay?"

"Sure," smiled Gertrude. She was too buoyant to even notice or care if there was a possible rebuke in Afosua's last words.

Gertrude crept beneath the sheets on her bed and stared up at the ceiling. Sleep would not come to her, nor did she want it to. She didn't want to miss a thing on this trip, even if it was just the buzz of traffic outside her window.

*****

Four men stood to greet Afosua and Gertrude as they approached the table reserved for the group. After introductions, they all sat and ordered dinner. Carsten Amsel was the head of marketing for the project. He had boyish good looks, with deep blue eyes and a dimpled smile. He seemed harmless and trustworthy, perfect for someone in marketing. Dietrich Blau and Simon Frei were responsible for anatomizing *synsepalum dulcificum*. They could have been brothers. Each had mousy brown hair and they were wearing near matching ensembles of light checkered shirts and wrinkled khakis. Being lab technicians, Afosua guessed that this might have been the most they had dressed up in weeks. Lucas Gottlieb's job was to assess the risks involved in the project. They would be working with him most and, more importantly, had to convince him that Phillips & Boakye were the actuaries that could give him the most accurate assessment. He said little over dinner, obviously studying the two women. Dietrich, on the other hand, was full of questions.

"You'll have to forgive me, but I am a bit surprised to see the two of you here," he said sipping his wine.

"How do you mean?" asked Afosua

"Well, and forgive me if this sounds ignorant, but you're two women... two AFRICAN women, here on a business trip when the men are at home. It's very odd, don't you think?"

Afosua felt her forehead knot uncontrollably. Before she got out a word, Gertrude interjected.

"Findest du es seltsam, dass eine afrikanische Frau so gut Deutsch spricht?" she asked.

Dietrich looked at her quizzically.

"Ja... I mean, yes –"

Gertrude chuckled.

"You really ought to get out of the lab more," she teased without mercy. "Africa is no longer the dark continent that you see in the movies. We drive cars, wear clothes and everything. And occasionally, we women do travel without men for business."

A hush came over the table. Afosua held her breath. The project was over before it began. It was Carsten who broke the spell and laughed uproariously.

"Touché! This is true!" he said, smiling at Gertrude. "I think before the end of your trip, you will have taught us many things about Africa, or about Ghana in particular."

He held her gaze over the rim of his wine glass as he sipped. Gertrude flushed slightly and looked away. The moment went unnoticed by Afosua, who was still silently fuming over Dietrich's ignorance. She stabbed her salad with indignation, eager now to go to bed. She was so focused on assaulting her food that she hadn't noticed Lucas leaning in to talk to her. She jumped when she heard his low voice in her ear.

"I'd like to have a private word with you after dinner."

Oh no. What could he possibly want?

****

Lucas stood and asked Afosua to join him at the bar. She dutifully followed him.

"Your colleague is very pretty."

"Gertrude? Yes, I suppose she is."

"I hope she is not equally naïve."

Afosua glanced back at Lucas. She had been watching Gertrude and Carsten get cozier and cozier, slowly excluding the other two men from their conversation.

"And what would she have to be wary of? I'm not sure why her naiveté would come into question in present company."

Lucas shifted his weight on the bar stool he was sitting on and traced his finger against the dark oak surface of the bar.

"I've seen this before," he confided. "With Carsten, I mean. He's indiscriminate. Clients, contracts, it doesn't matter the business relationship. He finds a woman he's attracted to and beds her for sport. I don't think your friend is equipped to handle that."

"I see," mused Afosua. "Don't you think you are being disloyal to *your* colleague, seeing as you are blacklisting him so unreservedly?"

Lucas shook his head.

"Perhaps I am being disloyal to Carsten, yes... but my allegiances lie with my company and its interests."

Afosua nodded in understanding. She appreciated his pragmatic approach.

"I'll tell you one other thing," Dietrich continued. "I consider this trip a formality. I have already decided that Phillips & Boakye is the actuary that would provide Deutsch Tech the best quality of work. I don't believe any other firm in Ghana can provide us with the level of intelligent analysis that yours can, from what I've researched. Your job from here on is to not prove me wrong. I would hate for something as small as a temporary dalliance to ruin all our long term objectives. I hope I make myself clear?"

"Understood," Afosua replied, picking up her drink. "I think it's time we retired for the evening, Mr. Gottlieb. Thank you for this chat."

Afosua walked over to the table and motioned for Gertrude to join her.

"Good night gentlemen and thank you for a wonderful evening. We will see you all in the morning."

As the rest of the party stood to leave as well, Lucas cast Afosua a reconfirming glance. She kept her face towards the direction of the elevator and strode towards it. It was time to get her mind refocused.

******

The train ride from Frankfurt to Dresden was going to take four hours. Carsten, Lucas and the rest of the team were scheduled to meet Afosua and Gertrude at the lab the next day, giving them a chance to tour the facility and hear from Deutsch Tech's engineers. Whether or not their operation would be successful in Ghana depended on the infrastructure they would require. Afosua knew she would have to develop some sort of work-around if their goals were too ambitious.

As soon as they were seated, she handed Gertrude a portfolio.

"Why are we here, Gertrude?"

"To make an assessment for DeutschTech Labs?" she replied nervously.

"Exactly. To make an assessment," Afosua confirmed. "We are not here to play games – romantic games in particular. We both have a lot to lose if this goes wrong."

"What do you mean?"

"Oh come on!" Afosua hissed. "Don't make me spell it out for you. I mean you and Carsten and your thin attempts at hiding your flirtation. Don't mess with him, don't sleep with him, don't do anything for him! He is our client and nothing else, okay?"

Gertrude nodded quietly. She wouldn't have minded the reprimand, if only Afosua had kept her tone a little lower. Everyone could hear her! The two rode in stony silence, faking a concentrated interest in the details of the project. It pained Afosua to start their trip off this way but she knew she had to steer the ship vigilantly.

*****

Deutsch Tech Labs (DTL) was a sprawling facility which looked deceptively smaller than it was, camouflaged as it was by indigenous trees and bushes. The German company was researching everything from how to grow tomatoes in frigid temperatures to isolating proteins in shrimp to regenerate human cells. The tour of the facility took two hours to complete, and both Afosua and Gertrude ended up regretting their decision to wear pumps. By the time they got to the conference room to hear DTL's prospectus for their Ghanaian venture, both sank gratefully into the swivel chairs closest to the door.

Gertrude began furiously scribbling notes, while Afosua focused her attention on the spatial limitations the project would face. It had not escaped her that DTL might have to extend its reach into Ghana's neighboring countries to achieve the volume of product it needed. As the facility manager droned on about the company's many accomplishments, Afosua couldn't help but wish this conversation was taking place in Accra or Kumasi... anywhere in Ghana. Her country had enough resources and intelligence to build labs to create medicines at home. Yet, once again, foreigners were preparing to make use of the natural bounty that she and her countryman frivolously discarded.

As if reading her thoughts, the facility director asked her a pointed question.

"Do you use *asaa*, Ms. Gyemfi?"

She raised her eyebrows and stared at him, almost in a panic.

"Me? No – although I heard it was very popular many years ago, mostly in the villages."

"Ahh. I see. We call it *Die Wunderbeere* – the wonder berry. People have tried for years to export it, but it has such a short shelf life. We think we can overcome that… with your help of course."

"Yes. Of course."

She felt like a sellout and she hated it. Still, any investment in Ghana was good investment, or so the government kept saying.

Their guide shut down his projector and ended his presentation. "Shall we break for lunch? This way please."

"*Danke*," said Gertrude softly, picking up her purse to follow him out.

Afosua noticed the change in Gertrude's demeanor during lunch. She did not want her to retreat back into her shell, not after she had started out so well. As her colleague poked at her chicken, Afosua touched her arm lightly.

"Look, I'm sorry if I was cruel on the train. I just don't want use to lose sight of the reason we are here. We have a lot of people back home depending on us – and at least one that is expecting us to fail. Can you understand that?"

Gertrude nodded.

"Let's start all over again, please? You're doing fabulously, and from one woman to another, I want to see you carry on that way."

This made Gertrude smile.

"Very well," she breathed. "I guess now would be a good time to tell you that you ordered pickled pig ears, not roasted ham. I was going to watch you squirm – and possibly vomit when it arrived… and then laugh at you privately."

"Oh chale. You're wicked ooo!"

"I guess that makes us both even then!"

The two women laughed and reordered Afosua's lunch. Afosua was sure that everything was going to be okay.

Five days later Afosua and Gertrude wrapped up their proposal and recommendation to the Deutsch Tech group. Though the men didn't say so, the trip had been a resounding success, judging from the smiles and chatter that filled the boardroom. All that was left for the pair to do was to get their findings back to Phillips & Boakye so that the company could proceed.

Lucas Gottlieb approached Afosua from behind and cleared his throat. She stopped packing her briefcase and turned to face him.

"Excellent job, Ms. Gyemfi," he said, commending her. "I'm pleased to see your team was able to stay focused."

"Yes," she smiled patronizingly. "That was why we are here, after all."

"I wonder… if I might take you to dinner? Maybe start our dealings on a more friendly note from here on out?"

Afosua glanced down at Lucas' left hand and took note of his ring. There may have been many things she did, but going out unaccompanied with a married business partner who was so inextricably linked to her success was not one of them. She didn't care if his intentions were pure or not.

"You know, I'd better not. We have an early flight back to Accra tomorrow and I really need to spend my evening typing up my notes."

Lucas smiled.

"Very astute, Ms. Gyemfi. I believe I made the right choice with Phillips & Boakye. If everyone in your firm has this level of integrity, I'd say we're in good shape."

The subject of integrity caused Afosua to grimace. She thought of Harold Boakye. His integrity was certainly to be questioned.

She reached out to shake Lucas' hand and bid him goodbye.

"*Auf Wiedersehen*, Herr Gottlieb."

"*Auf Wiedersehen*, Frau Gyemfi."

Gertrude and Afosua walked out to the shuttle that was waiting to take them back to their hotel. As soon as they got into the vehicle, Afosua let her weight settle into the seat and sighed with relief.

"Thank God that's over!"

*****

The sun had begun to set over Dresden, and Gertrude was looking wistfully outside of the window. Afosua stopped typing long enough to glace at her.

"Gertrude, do you want to explore the city?"

The younger woman brightened.

"Yes, actually, I do!"

"Better you than me," said Afosua. "You'll be right at home. You go on. I'm just finishing up these notes for Mark."

Gertrude already had her purse and had her hand on the knob.

"I'll call you if I need anything!" she yelled, now halfway down the hall.

She never knew when she'd have this opportunity to see this city again.

Once outside the double doors of the hotel, Gertrude looked around and decided to turn right. There was a small shop selling maps and snacks, and she figured she could use both for the evening. After she made her purchase, she saw a familiar figure approach her. It was Carsten.

"You've been avoiding me," he said, smiling impishly.

"No, no! Not at all."

"Don't lie, my dear. I'm in marketing and I can sniff insincerity immediately," he teased. "You've scuttled off in every direction but towards mine since we had dinner that first night."

"Yes... fine. It's true. I came here for work, and I had to stay on course."

"And now that work is over?"

Gertrude paused and thought about it.

"Well I suppose I could have a bit of fun. Will you show me your town?"

Carsten smiled.

"It would be my pleasure."

Carsten and Gertrude strode leisurely through the streets of the old city. Gertrude could hardly contain her excitement, and commented often on the massive stone cathedrals, museums and lamp posts. Carsten found her girlish enthusiasm endearing. Feeling a little bolder, he took her by the waist and walked hip-to-hip with her. Gertrude did not rebuff his advances. She was intoxicated by Carsten's cool scent and hypnotizing brogue. Everything about him made her feel safe, even though she hardly knew the man.

When it was dark, they found a bench and sat at the banks of the River Elbe.

"My father was an engineer," said Carsten. "We've lived all over the world – Asia, Australia and anywhere you can think of in Europe. Finally when I went to university I decided that I would settle in Germany and try to plant some roots."

"I can understand that... wanting to belong," said Gertrude, folding her hands across her lap. Carsten moved closer and put his arm around her shoulder.

"You look cold. Do you want to go back to your hotel?"

Gertrude shook her head. There was nothing for her to do back there, and this was the most fun she'd had so far. Suddenly, a slight drizzle began to fall.

"Come on," ordered Carsten. "I can't send you back to Accra sick. I'd never forgive myself. We'll catch a cab to my place. I don't live too far from here."

"Alright," said Gertrude, trying to sound confident. She was unsure of what she would do if she was alone with this man, but her feet didn't give her a chance to make a different decision. Before she knew it, they were in Carsten's apartment.

He gave her a quick tour before offering a glass of wine.

"I'll just have water."

"Do you think I'm trying to take advantage of you?" he chuckled.

"I don't know. Maybe...Yes."

"Look, we don't have to do anything that makes you uncomfortable, okay?"

His blue eyes looked at her kindly and sincerely. She felt relieved.

"Ok," Gertrude said, letting out a breath. "Can we just talk? Your life sounds so fascinating, so different from mine."

"I'm sure your life is perfect." Carsten kissed her softly on the cheek. "I think you're perfect."

Gertrude led him to the sofa and took off her shoes. He slowly began stroking her hair and telling her his life's story. Before she knew it, she had fallen asleep with her head on his shoulder. It was the most intimate moment she'd ever shared with a man.

*****

The next morning, Gertrude woke in a panic. She had to get to the airport and she had no idea where she was.

"Good morning!" said Carsten cheerfully.

"Morning, morning." Gertrude was looking for her shoes. "I have to get back to the hotel quickly, or I'll miss my flight."

"You have a little time before you have to leave," objected Carsten. "Sit. I made you a light breakfast."

He handed her a plate heaped with sausage, ham and eggs. Gertrude stared at the imposing bounty and picked up her knife, slicing her ham into thin, rectangular strips. Carsten watched her pensively as she ate.

"That's interesting."

"What is?" she asked, shoveling the food into her mouth as genteelly as possible.

"The way you cut your meat. Do many Ghanaians cut it that way?"

"I don't know. What makes you ask?"

"It's just that when I was a kid we lived in Ghana as well. Remember? I told you last night. You might have drifted to sleep by then. I hardly remember it though. I was only about five when we left."

Gertrude stopped cutting her food and chewed her food pensively.

"Whereabouts did you live in Ghana?"

"I don't recall. But I do remember our housemaid. Lovely woman. Her name was Serena, Celia…"

"*Cecelia*?"

"Yes! That's it. She cut her food the same way you did. She called it 'designing food.' I always thought that was funny, like she was comparing food to cutting cloth or something."

Carsten chuckled as he recalled his childhood memory. Gertrude sat frozen, suddenly feeling sick to her stomach with a ghastly realization: she had just spent the entire night with her brother.

******

Afosua stood impatiently outside the departure gate. The flight was being called when Gertrude ran up with her carry-on bag.

"Where have you been!" she scolded. "You almost missed the flight and..."

She stopped her tirade when she noticed how pallid Gertrude was. The woman was trembling and pale.

"Are you alright Gertie? Did you get caught in the rain last night?"

Gertrude swallowed deeply.

"I'm fine. I'm fine. They're calling our seats now. Let's just get out of here."

Afosua looked at her with concern and then decided to let it go. Whatever it was that troubling Gertrude, she figured that was mature enough to handle it.

Nothing could have been further from the truth.

Cecelia waited nervously for her daughter to arrive back home in a taxi. She had been cooking since morning, and most of the food was settling at room temperature now. Most of the money that she earned had gone towards educating and clothing Gertrude, and it had never occurred to her that she might invest in a microwave. It seemed like an unnecessary expense – until now. Her daughter was returning from *abrochi* and she was going to be greeted with cold food! There was nothing for it now. She went to the window and waited.

When a red and yellow taxi pulled up to their small home, Cecelia's heart leapt. She dashed to the road's edge and hugged Gertrude tightly.

"Akwaaba!" she gushed, grabbing both of Gertrude's bags. She bolted towards the house like a frisky pet. This was the longest she'd been separated from her child and she finally felt at ease now that her baby was home.

The younger woman paid the taxi driver and caught up with her mother.

"No, no, Ma. I'll carry the bags."

"Nonsense. Do you think I got old in the one week you were gone?" chided Cecelia. "How can I let you come from abroad and carry your own bags?"

Gertrude knew there was no point in arguing and let her mother do as she pleased. She didn't have the strength to fight her anyway.

She slipped off her shoes at the door and sat on a wooden bench in the narrow corridor leading into their home. Cecelia looked behind her, surprised that her daughter was not following her to the dining room. Gertrude's head was buried in her lap, her shoulders rising and falling silently.

"Oh dear. You're so tired, eh?" said Cecelia compassionately. "Come with me. I've cooked you so much food, it will make you feel better."

Gertrude looked at her mother with red rimmed eyes. It was a look Cecelia had never seen before. It frightened her.

"Gertrude, what's the matter?"

"I met a man while I was in Germany, Ma," she replied through a tight throat.

Cecelia steadied herself for bad news.

"Did he hurt you?"

"No. He didn't hurt me."

"Then why are you crying?"

"Because I almost fell in love with him!" Gertrude sobbed uncontrollably.

"Ah. But what's wrong with that? You can call him and email him, and even invite him to Ghana if you like!"

Cecelia was beginning to get annoyed with her daughter. She was acting like a spoiled baby and ruining the elaborate welcome she had planned. Gertrude stopped crying and rested her head against the wall. She was deliberate when she spoke.

"Yes, Ma. You're right. I should invite him to Ghana. After all, my brother should know where I live, shouldn't he?"

"What do you mean 'your brother'? Who did you meet in Germany, Gertie?"

"Carsten, Ma. Carsten Amsel. Is he my brother? Am I right?"

Cecelia dropped to her knees and stared at her daughter. She didn't know what to say.

"It's time for us to talk, Ma," said Gertrude softly. "It's time for you to tell me everything."

Cecelia nodded and rose slowly to her feet. She held out her hand, silently urging Gertrude to take it. She pulled her precious daughter to her feet and led her past the dining room. The food could wait. It was no remedy for her daughter's broken heart.

*****

Naa Akweley sat with her feet tucked under her bottom on the sofa. She welcomed the glare of the afternoon sun, drawing strength from its warmth. Working on the plans for health spa had made her feel more invigorated than she had in a long time. Stacks of paper were strewn around the room, filled with ideas that seemed to be coming to her in furious spurts. When Afosua returned, she would ask her to let her use her laptop. Afosua had seemed so shaken before she left over something she'd read on it, and Naa didn't want to betray her trust by looking like she'd been snooping.

A key in the door snapped her from her thoughts.

"You're back!"

"Yes," said Afosua wearily. She instructed the watchman to leave her bags by the door and thanked him. When he was gone, she flopped onto the sofa next to Naa Akweley.

"Was it a bad trip?"

Afosua shook her head.

"Actually, no. We got the contract. And something strange happened with Gertrude but she won't say," she said pensively. "Doesn't matter though; we got the business, and I have a chance to show some real leadership in the company."

Naa Akweley nodded silently, stacking her papers into a neat pile.

"What's all this?" Afosua asked.

Naa broke into a wide grin.

"These are all my ideas for Dumbai," she said proudly. "When you're rested, we can go over them."

"Sure!" Afosua said keenly. "And how are *you*? How's the baby?"

Naa rubbed her belly absently.

"The baby is fine. Moving a lot now more lately. So much in fact that I feel like he might try to make an early arrival."

The thought of having a baby alone frightened her. She knew that she couldn't count on Afosua's generosity forever, no matter what her friend said. She would have to sort out her life somehow, but she just couldn't bring herself to think about it. The idea of bringing up a child without his father weighed heavily on her spirit. What if the boy resented her?

What would other little kids say about him when he went to school? She swept these unpleasant thoughts from her mind, set her papers on the coffee table and looked up. Someone was knocking on the door.

"I asked Joyce to bring me some tea a while ago," Naa Akweley said. "I bet that's her."

She swung the door open and stepped aside to let Joyce in...but Ian Blankson was standing in the doorway instead.

"Wh-what are you doing here?" Naa Akweley stammered.

"Is that anyway to greet your husband?" Ian groused. "I've been looking for you for weeks, wife."

Afosua leapt out of her chair and blocked the door with her body.

"How the fuck did you find my house?" she snarled. "How did you know she was here?"

Ian feigned shock and clicked his tongue disapprovingly.

"Such language from a lady! And to a man of God, too. It's not becoming at all... but what would one expect from a whore who doesn't know her place?"

"Ian... please," begged Naa Akweley helplessly.

Afosua glared at him in utter disgust.

"The good thing is, I DO know my place. And this is my home. Get the hell off my property or I will have you thrown off!"

"I'll leave, but not without my wife," Ian said simply. "Your absence has been very inconvenient for me, Naa. The excuse that you've gone on a retreat is no longer practical. From where the congregation sits, it's beginning to look like you've abandoned your husband and your church."

"You and your congregation can go straight to hell!" screeched Afosua. She had suddenly acquired an acute hatred for the sound of Ian's voice. "What have you and your flock done for her but beat her down and run her ragged?"

Afosua's shrieking summoned her mother and Joyce, who was carrying a tray of tea and watching the fierce exchange from a safe distance. The girls in the area would not believe this when she told them!

"What's going on here?" demanded Elizabeth. "Who is this man?"

"This is Ian Blankson, Mama. Naa Akweley's husband... and we can handle this."

Elizabeth recognized the man immediately. She gently pushed him aside and yanked her daughter's arm.

"Afosua, this man is an important man! He's godly! How dare you treat him in this way. Shame on you!"

"This 'man' is a pig, Ma! And you know nothing about this!"

"Afosua, if Pastor Blankson has business with his wife, you have to let him speak to her privately about this. You cannot interfere in someone else's marriage."

"Oh you're one to talk!" Afosua spat at her mother.

Elizabeth recoiled at the thinly veiled insult. She had always known that Afosua held secret resentment towards her because she had been her father's mistress, but this was the first time her daughter had ever made reference to it.

173

Elizabeth almost lost her footing on the step as she retreated in stunned silence.

"Naa Akweley, this wise woman is right," said Ian, seizing on the moment. "We have to discuss this ourselves. Alone. You are my *wife* – and I am your husband. I am the head of our household but you are the body. What use is the head without the body? Can't you see I need you?"

Ian sounded so sincere and so convincing to Naa Akweley. Her baby began kicking wildly at the sound of his father's voice. Maybe it was time to end the charade. Perhaps it was time to go home.

Naa Akweley stepped out from behind the door and faced her husband.

"Will things be different?" she asked warily. "You know what I'm talking about."

Ian let out a short, sorrowful breath. He reached for her wrist and gently kissed her palm.

"Sweetheart, I know that I have been less than perfect, but I have been working on it. I promise that I will keep doing my best."

Ian kept his gaze downward as he spoke, only looking his wife in the eye when he had finished his speech. In those eyes, she saw a glimpse of the man she had fallen in love with years ago. She turned the corners of her mouth upward ever so slightly and silently followed him to the car. Afosua was aghast.

"Naa Akweley! Don't do this. Don't go!" she cried after her friend.

"I have to, Afos," she replied quietly. "He's my husband and he loves me. Why else would he come looking for me?"

"Because you're a pawn, *Naa*," Afosua spat. "We all know how this ends. It's not a mystery. Use your head woman. Please don't go!"

Naa Akweley was hurt by Afosua's assertion that she was not thinking. She would prove her wrong. Ian had come to find her; this had to be God's will. How else would he have known where she was? Naa Akweley stepped back to hug Afosua before she climbed into Ian's waiting car.

"Thank you for everything, my friend."

Afosua hugged her friend back tightly, trying in vain to prevent her departure. She clasped the back of Naa Akweley's neck, dislodging her hairclip... the same ruby red hair clip she had been wearing when she had seen Ian at the bakery over a week before. Her stomach knotted in that instant.

She had led Ian to Naa Akweley. This was all her fault.

Defeated, she watched the bumper of the pastor's sleek sedan disappear from view. The watchman swung the gate shut, terminating any hope that Naa Akweley might return. She filed past her mother who was watching her with hurt in her eyes. She had to make it right.

"Ma... I'm sorry, Mama. I never should have -"

Elizabeth held up her hand, her lips twisting as she strained her next words through them.

"Never speak to me that way again."

Afosua nodded meekly. None of this was her mother's fault. There was plenty of blame to go around, but the bulk of it did not belong at Elizabeth Anaan's feet. Afosua sunk into the spot on the sofa where Naa Akweley had been just moments before. It was still warm. She clutched the armrest and did something that felt uncomfortable but appropriate in the moment: she said a silent prayer for her friend.

Annette played nervously with the hem of her skirt and glanced occasionally at her lawyer. They had decided a few days ago that it would be Annette's best interest if she found somewhere more permanent to live and, more specifically, not with her council. She was hesitant to call Sophia but she had no one else to turn to. To Annette's relief, Sophia was eager to come and pick her up. Now it was time for her to focus on proving her innocence.

Lydia clicked through some files on her laptop, pensively rubbing her chin every so often. Finally, she leaned back in her chair and smiled at Annette.

"I think we're ready to go to trial," she grinned. "I just received an email from the clerk's office and Mr. Prah's lawyer has filed a motion to have this case fast-tracked. He wants to have an emergency hearing."

"Can he do that?" asked Annette anxiously.

"Of course he can!" laughed Lydia. "He's just banking on us not being ready."

"When do we appear in court?"

"In five days."

Annette blew out a long, slow breath and looked out of the window, searching for some phantom savior to magically appear. Lydia clicked her tongue disapprovingly.

"Have you been honest with me about everything?" she asked, piercing Annette with a quizzical stare over the rim of her glasses.

"Yes! Of course…"

"Then you have nothing to worry about," she said, rising from her desk. "Come with me. We're going out for lunch."

Annette hesitated.

"I thought you said attorneys and clients shouldn't mingle so casually."

"And we're not," replied Lydia. "It's a working lunch. There's something I want you to see."

*****

The two women walked to a road side kiosk and sat on a bench. Lydia brought over some roasted plantains and groundnuts and handed them to Annette, who looked at the fare curiously.

"Not very high class lawyer food, is this?" she sniffed.

"High class? No," agreed Lydia. "But it has all the essentials you will ever need – protein and carbohydrates. Plus, it's easily portable, and won't stain your clothes. All this 'designer' food that people are so obsessed with is terribly bad for you, fried rice and chicken and such."

Lydia threw a handful of roasted nuts into her mouth and chewed vigorously. Annette waited politely for her to say something else, but she never did. She cleared her throat to get Lydia's attention. She was looking in the distance, fixated on something – or someone.

"Did you bring me out here to have a conversation about culinary preferences?"

Lydia ignored the question.

"You see that girl over there, the one in the blue floral dress and short hair?"

Annette strained to find the child in question among the crowd of people milling about. Finally she spotted her, carrying a tray of bananas on her head.

"Yes. I see her. What about her?"

Lydia bit into a piece of plantain.

"I used to buy bananas from her all the time. You can't tell from here, but she's very pretty. She's smart, and hardworking."

Annette took stock of the child, who no longer blended in with the masses of faceless people crowding the street.

"She told me that she wanted to go to school, and she couldn't go to school until she had sold all her fruit," Lydia continued. "Someone obviously made her that promise – a mother, a father, some auntie charged with her care. So every day, I would come and buy all her bananas in the hope that I wouldn't see her the next day. But every day, I would pass this road on the way in to work and there she would be, with even more bananas. Until I realized I was doing her harm."

"How so?"

"It became clear that the more fruit she sold, the more her family would pile on her head to support them. She will never go beyond a class three education, and she will never live a life worthy of her hopes and dreams."

Annette chewed absently on her groundnuts, empathizing with the young street seller. How sad the girl's life must be.

"You're not much different from the street seller, you know."

"What?"

"Yes," continued Lydia. "To this day, you have let other people control your destiny and have handed over your future without a fight. Even if we win this court case against Mr. Prah, you will find yourself in the same or a similar situation again. There are a thousand Mr. Prah's waiting to take advantage of you. The difference between you and this little girl is that you are an adult. You have the power to do something about it; you just have refused to until now. It is time for you to become a full woman, otherwise all my work will be in vain."

Annette opened her mouth to object, but didn't. She quickly realized that Lydia was right and it would be wrong for her to argue with her.

"So do you ever buy bananas from the little girl, even occasionally?"

Lydia shook her head. And spoke quietly.

"No. I seem to have developed a strong disliking for bananas."

******

Afosua arrived at Tony's doorstep as the sun was going down. She was distraught over Naa Akweley's departure and ready to unleash all her fury on the closest target: Mr. Boakye.

Tony smiled and welcomed her in.

"Do you still have the files?"

"Yes, right here," Tony said, unlocking his brief case and handing it to her.

"Did you look over them?"

"Yes, I did. I needed to know whatever it is that had you so upset. At first it looked like standard stuff, maps and projections... but the deeper I looked, the more concerned I became about what I saw."

Afosua nodded.

"And why is that?"

"Something in the terminology just seemed familiar. I couldn't figure it out until I realized -"

"What?" said Afosua, holding her breath.

" – until I realized that this was the same prospectus format I use at Phillips & Boakye. There are millions of dollars in unaccounted revenue hidden in this proposal."

Afosua looked at Tony and waited for him to finish.

"Oh my God, is someone at P&B involved in something illegal?" he blurted suddenly.

"I believe they are," confirmed Afosua. "Either illegal or unethical, and I have to find out which."

"Phillips & Boakye have been my clients for a long time. I have always known them to be ethical. If someone is doing something to ruin that reputation, I'm going to help you unearth it."

Afosua could scarcely believe what she was hearing. She had taken a huge leap of faith in trusting Tony, not knowing if he would turn her in or not. He knew that something was wrong at the company, but how would he react when he found out that one of the owners was the culprit? Was he actually trustworthy? She buried her face in his chest, relieved to share at least part of this burden with another person. He lifted her chin and caressed her cheek.

"Hey. I told you before you left. Whatever I can do to help you, I will."

She kissed him softly in thanks. He returned the gesture with gentle care, realizing that the weight of her discovery must have been brutal for her. Despite Afosua's often brusque behavior, he could tell that she wanted affection. He smiled inwardly knowing that he was slowly winning his battle to give it to her. He rocked her gently in his brawny embrace.

"Will you make love to me?" she whispered.

"Of course," he murmured back.

Tony lifted Afosua's curvy frame and carried her to his home office. Something about the whir of a sleeping laptop always made their sex better. Afosua allowed herself to be plied by his skilled hands as he undressed them both. He smelled like soap and aftershave, and Afosua was heady with the scent of him. She sighed loudly when he began to suck her nipples, coaxing them until they stood like erect peaks. She had truly missed him while she was away and the realization that they were alone, undisturbed and together sent a violent surge of wetness through her. She took command, manipulating Tony into a sitting position on his office chair. She slid onto his massive erection, lifting her hips slightly and rhythmically until they were both glistening with sweat and the room was filled with the heavy musk of their lovemaking. Tony slid his hands beneath her soft buttocks, spreading them just enough so that he find himself within deeper in her. The faint change in tempo caused Afosua to cum quickly. She began to sob quietly and rested her head on his dark shoulders.

"It's okay, my love," Tony whispered, rubbing the small of her back. "It's okay."

Monday morning came sooner than Annette had anticipated. She walked bravely up the few steps leading into the local magistrate's house at Kanda and waited for her lawyer to appear in the foyer. Sophia had gone to find parking, leaving Annette alone and exposed. Dark clouds had begun to gather outside, threatening lightning and torrential rain by the time the morning was out; but the gloom outside hardly rivaled the desolation looming over her spirit.

The sound of familiar footsteps pricked her attention. Annette whipped around, coming face to face with Kwame Prah. He reached out to stroke her forearm in greeting.

"Hello my dear."

Annette snatched her arm away from the reach of her tormentor. He feigned surprise.

His tone was mocking. "Ei. Why so testy? After all we've been through together? And we have far more yet to go, my dear."

Annette glared at her husband icily. Lydia's words about letting others control her life sprang into her head, and she felt a wave of heat wash over her. She was shaking with fury.

"Is there a reason you are talking to my client?"

Lydia Oppong had materialized behind Mr. Prah, starling the elderly man.

"Is there a reason you're talking to my client, Mr. Prah?" she repeated.

"Barrister Oppong… I didn't see you there. What? Can't a man have a friendly chat with his wife?" he asked innocently.

Lydia grimaced.

"I don't think you need me to tell you that you can't, Mr. Prah. Annette, shall we?"

Lydia showed Annette into courtroom, which was already half full of spectators. The fast track courts gave the illusion of informality, despite the fact that the accused's life and livelihood hung in the balance. For Annette, it was all very overwhelming. Although miserable, her life had been predictable so far. At least she could count on that. She looked around for Lydia for comfort, but her lawyer was already seated at the bar with the prosecution and was shuffling through her notes. Annette drew long, calming breaths and found a speck of dirt on the floor to focus her attention on. She realized that looking downward – and frightened by implication – might also have made her look guilty. But she was much more afraid of going crazy if she dared to look around the room.

Two women sitting in the audience began to talk about her, not bothering to hush their voices.

"This foolish girl," one sneered, "how can she treat her husband that way? Look at how he's cared for her all these years."

The other sucked her teeth in agreement.

"Don't mind her. This is how these *half-co* girls behave. They think they are better than anyone else."

"I just want to knock her head," the other replied in malice.

Annette knew she would not help her case if she responded. She sighed and struggled to hold on to what little composure she had left. To her left she saw Mr. Prah had found a seat as well, smiling victoriously at everyone in the room. He was so powerful. How would she possibly win? She felt like she was tied to a rock, battling unabating waves of defeat.

"Hey you," said a female voice, tapping her on the shoulder. It was Afosua.

"Hi!" Annette whispered. "Thank you for coming!"

Afosua smiled reassuringly at her.

"I will stay as long as I can. But trust me, you're in good hands with Lydia."

Annette's eyes filled with tears. She nodded her appreciation. The small courtroom was now filling quickly, and Sophia had found a seat by the back door. With her small sect of supporters in the room, Annette felt a lot more consoled. A booming voice cut into the air, grabbing everyone's attention.

"All rise! The Honorable Judge Gyempoh presiding!"

A heavyset man with a black robe and white judge's tie entered the room from his chamber and ascended to the high wooden desk. He sat down without looking at anyone in the room and took up the case file that had been left by the clerk, a young woman in a batik skirt and plain white top. Annette noted that the girl had way too much pomade in her hair, which made her look greasy and dishonest.

"We will hear opening statements from the prosecution first," said the magistrate.

"Thank you m'lord," boomed Sylvester Acquah, Mr. Prah's lawyer. "M'lord, we are here today to charge a certain Mrs. Annette Prah for the theft of goods and a sum of money totaling ₡50,000. We will prove that Mrs. Prah committed fraud, forgery and adultery and as such has caused my client physical and financial harm. We will seek re-compensation and punishment for these crimes, according to the court's direction."

"Thank you Mr. Acquah. Ms. Oppong?"

Lydia Oppong stood and furrowed her brow. Her wide stance made her appear twice her normal size, and she appeared to levitate and hover over the room. She was fearsome to behold. Her voice was low and commanding, her eyes engaging anyone who dared to meet them.

"Thank you my lord. The charges against Mrs. Prah are completely false and completely fabricated. We intend to prove Mrs. Prah's innocence, and furthermore prove that it is Mr. Prah who is guilty of theft and guilty of stealing something worth far more than ₡50,000 – an entire lifetime from Annette Prah. You will hear riveting testimony that will vacate my client of any wrongdoing, and will most certainly find her not guilty of the prevaricating charges of theft and fraud. We are confident that if there is any punishment directed by the court, it will not be levied upon Annette Prah."

The judge banged his gavel as the court room erupted in a low grumble.

"Silence," he commanded. "The prosecution will call its first witness."

Mr. Acquah called Kwame Prah to the stand, asking him to state his name and nature of his business. Annette looked at her husband in disgust, as he gleefully rehashed the same speech that he always gave when he was asked how he became a man of fortune. She knew he was finished when the tempo of his voiced rose to a crescendo and he uttered the words "self-made man."

"And how did you come to meet your wife, Mr. Prah?"

"Well," croaked the septuagenarian, "she was a student at my son's school, and always used to hang about whenever I came to visit him. She did all she could to get nearer to me, and I took pity on her. Her own parents never came to visit her, and I kind of adopted her. In time, she expressed that she loved me. I myself was a widower and had not had the comfort of a woman in years. She seduced me. She's very beautiful, so it was hard for me to resist."

"That is a LIE!" Annette screamed.

"Order!" cried the judge.

"You know fucking well that is a lie, you low life!" she yelled louder.

"Barrister Oppong, control your client, or I will have her removed!" the judge warned.

Lydia looked sternly at Annette, who sat down meekly. Her heart was pounding. Sylvester Acquah raised his eyebrows in mock surprise, looking around the room and playing on the spectators' emotions. He solicited pity for the elderly man with his glance.

"Mr. Prah, do continue," he said gently. "Please tell us about your life with Mrs. Prah."

"Well, she was insatiable," replied Kwame Prah. "I work very hard, and late at night she would come into my room and demand sex from me. I'm old, as you can see – but I did my best to satisfy her. I have taken much medication to make me strong... if you get my meaning... but it was never enough. Eventually, she began to pull away from me."

Lydia glared at Annette, warning her with her eyes to keep silent. Annette sat on her hands, her fingers twisting in revulsion. The thought of all those nights spent with Kwame Prah slithering over her made her feel ill. She was beyond incensed. She was in utter disbelief.

"Mr. Prah, can you tell us about the night that your wife ran off with your money?"

"Certainly," he replied congenially. "I had just retired from my company, and I announced that we would be going away together for a year. I thought the time away from Accra would strengthen our relationship. I thought she would be pleased, but she looked so angry that night at the banquet. To my dismay, I woke the following morning to find her room vacant. She had taken only a few things – some clothing and a hand bag. It was then that I checked the safe in my study and found that the money was stolen, in cash."

"And how would she have access to this safe?"

"I have no secrets with my wife," said Mr. Prah simply. "She knows everything. I never imagined she would steal from me and hurt my family so much."

"Thank you, Mr. Prah."

The judge asked Lydia if she wanted to cross-examine the witness.

"No your honor," she replied.

Annette gasped in horror. She wanted Lydia to make him tell the truth! Make him take back everything he had said! Afosua rubbed her friend's back, willing her to trust the lawyer.

"The prosecution wishes to call Mr. Jerry Mensah to the stand!"

A thin man in silver-rimmed spectacles took the witness stand. After he was sworn in, he sat cautiously at the edge of his wooden seat. Jerry Mensah was Mr. Prah's IT director at the shipping firm. He had never really liked Annette. He thought she was too high-minded and full of herself. He especially did not like the way she treated his boss... although he had never seen them in public. Still, he assumed that she must be a horrible woman to be so young and to pursue a man who was old enough to be her grandfather. He looked condescendingly at her from the witness box. Now he would get her.

"Mr. Mensah, can you tell us what you have discovered from the accused's email communication?"

"Yes, sir I can," began Jerry. "I discovered three years' worth of communication between Mrs. Prah and one individual."

"And what was the nature of these messages?"

"Amorous. As though two people were in love. There was constant talk of meeting times and rendezvous," confirmed Jerry Mensah.

"And were you able to discover the identity of this individual?"

Jerry shook his head.

"Unfortunately, no. The email address of the recipient was encrypted and displays only as a series of letters and numbers."

"I see," said Mr. Acquah, stroking his chin. "But in your opinion, these emails were certainly between a man and a woman... two lovers you say?"

"Objection. Prosecution is leading," Lydia bellowed.

"Sustained."

"No further questions. Thank you, Mr. Mensah."

Sylvester Acquah sat smugly at the bar. Lydia rose and faced Jerry Mensah, smiling demurely.

"Mr. Mensah, thank you for being here. Tell us, are you in law enforcement?" she asked sweetly.

"No."

"And Mr. Prah is your employer?"

"That is correct."

"When you 'came across' these emails, where were you?"

"I was in my office," said Jerry Mensah proudly.

"And are you the owner of the email account in which these communications are contained?"

"No, of course not. Annette Prah is." He cast the younger woman a disapproving glance.

"And did you have her permission to access her private messages?"

"Ehh… no." Jerry was beginning to get nervous.

"Oh? So how did you get access, with whose permission?"

Jerry looked nervously at his boss, who sat stone-faced.

"If it wasn't with Annette Prah's consent, then surely it was by the request of someone here? I would hate to think that the prosecution would ask you to illegally obtain files."

Jerry Mensah looked petrified. He hadn't imagined that the method with which he got the data would come into question.

"Did Mr. Prah ask you to hack his wife's account?"

"I – I can't say," he stuttered, unsure.

"Because if he did, I would like to draw the court's attention to the fact that accessing another person's personal data by an individual not acting in the capacity of law enforcement, is quite illegal. Now we have to ask ourselves: Mr. Mensah did you access this information illegally? On the other hand, if you DID access these messages legally, we might infer that that would make YOU the owner of the encrypted email address – correct?"

Jerry Mensah muttered something under his breath.

"Would you repeat that sir? The court could not hear you," barked Lydia.

"I said I would never sleep with that cheating tramp, let alone email her about it!" he said louder.

"Then I believe you've answered my question," said Lydia haughtily. "You may step down, Mr. Mensah."

Jerry Mensah trudged away from the witness stand, avoiding eye contact with his boss. Mr. Prah sat in enraged silence.

"Your honor, I move to have this 'evidence' rendered inadmissible as it was illegally obtained. Any subsequent emails sent to and from Mrs. Prah gathered in this manner cannot be used to confirm or deny any alleged infidelity."

"Granted," replied the judge, nodding to the clerk.

Lydia took her seat at the bar, stacked her papers and shifted them to the left. No one but Afosua knew what elation she was feeling right now. Above anything else, Lydia loved to win, and this round had been very simple. Behind her, Afosua saw the judge look at his watch.

"The court will have a recess for lunch," he announced. "We will reconvene in two hours."

He banged his gavel and stood, lifting the rest of the courtroom with him. When he had retreated to his chambers, Lydia strode over to Annette's seat. Her face was stern.

"Lydia… I – I'm so sorry for my outbursts. I promise, it won't happen again…"

Lydia cut her off.

"You haven't been completely honest with me," she said tersely.

Annette cast her gaze downward. She knew what Lydia was asking. Sophia walked up to the two of them in that instant, looking worried. If Mr. Prah had unearthed their emails, there was no telling what else he could do. It was time to come clean.

"Come on," Sophia instructed to two women. "We need to find some place private to talk."

Afosua left the courthouse as soon as the recess was announced and went back to her office. She prayed that Mr. Boakye would be out when she arrived. Someone must have been listening in the heavens: only Gertrude and Mark Phillips were there when she pulled in.

"Hey Gertrude," she said breathlessly. "Where is Mark?"

Gertrude pointed towards to break room without looking up from her computer screen. She had been sullen since they returned from Germany, but Afosua didn't have time to find out why. As far as she knew, there was no reason for Gertrude to be upset about anything concerning the trip, and her sulking only made her look childish. Mark was pouring a cup of tea when Afosua pushed open the door.

"Ms. Gyemfi! What a pleasant surprise," he said congenially. "I didn't expect you to be in the office so soon after your trip."

"I wanted to make sure all of our paperwork and findings were submitted before I left."

"Left? Where are you going?"

Afosua rubbed the back of her neck, which had suddenly formed a knot. She looked at the main entrance nervously, fearful that Harold might walk in at any moment.

"I have some leave coming to me and I thought that I might take it now. I'll be out of the office for the next two weeks."

"Do you have plans for something fun?" asked Mark casually, sipping his drink.

"No," said Afosua. "Not fun… but very pressing and very personal."

"Then I won't keep you from it."

He extended his hand to shake hers and congratulated her on the hard work she had put in on the DeutschTech project.

"You've certainly earned the time away," he smiled. "You and Gertrude did a fantastic job."

"Thank you, sir."

"By the way, do you know what's wrong with her?" asked Mark, full of concern. "She's been acting so strangely since you both got back. Very withdrawn. Did something happen?"

"Not that I know of," replied Afosua, thinking back. "Perhaps she just wanted to stay longer. Travelling abroad can have that affect."

Mark looked a little more relaxed with that explanation.

"I suppose you're right."

Afosua waved goodbye with her cell phone in hand.

"If you need me, just call me. I'll still be available to answer work questions," she advised.

Mark smiled and nodded wordlessly at her retreating back. He knew he had made a good hire in Afosua Gyemfi, no matter what Harold Boakye had to say to the contrary. Where was Harold anyway? It wasn't like him not to be in the office at the hour. Mark poured a little cream in his cup and went back to his desk and chuckled as he thought about his co-founder. There was no telling what Harold was up to!

******

"What is going on?" demanded Lydia, unbuttoning her black robe and laying it on the back seat of her car. She stared intently at Annette, who was shifting from foot to foot.

"Have you been sleeping with another man?" she asked again.

"No!" Annette wailed. "I haven't."

"Then what is this business that Mr. Prah is trying to pull with clandestine emails?" Lydia whispered in rage. "I was completely taken off guard. Who is this alleged affair supposed to have been with, heh?"

"With me."

Lydia whipped around and gawked at Sophia.

"I'm sorry... what?"

"Annette has been having an affair with me," repeated Sophia. "If that's the proper term for it."

Lydia stared at the two women for a brief while before bursting into a long, deep chuckle.

"Well, Annette Prah. Aren't you a piece of work," she finally said when her fit of laughter had subsided.

"You... you're not angry?"

"Yes, of course I am. I asked you to be honest with me about everything. I don't understand why you didn't tell me *this*."

"I guess I thought it wasn't relevant. I'm being accused of theft, not adultery... and ..."

"And you were a bit ashamed, weren't you?"

Annette looked at Sophia before turning her head away and nodding.

"I honestly didn't know how you would take it."

"Oh please," Lydia scoffed. "We've all been in boarding school. This is type of relationship is nothing new."

Sophia slid close to Annette and put her hand in hers.

"So what do we do now?" asked Annette.

"The obvious thing," said Lydia with a sly grin. "We tell the court the truth... when the time is right."

She tightened the strap of her purse around her shoulder.

"Come on. I'm starving. I see a plantain roaster not too far from here."

*****

Tony was pacing outside of the Lands Commission, anxiously looking at his phone. He put it in his pocket when Afosua finally pulled up ten minutes later. She hopped out of her car and bounded up the few steps leading into the building.

"You should have called me to tell me you were late."

"Sorry," she muttered. "I ran out of credit."

"You really ought to get on a monthly plan," he sniffed. "A professional woman has no business running out of credit!"

"Yeah, I'll take that up with MTN or Vodafone ASAP. As you can imagine, it's high on my to-do list," she replied sarcastically. "Shall we?"

Chastised, Tony opened the wide wooden doors for Afosua and allowed her to walk in ahead of him. She immediately felt bad for being short with him. He was doing her a huge favor, setting up this meeting with the clerk at the land title registry. It was a favor that could jeopardize his own position if it got out that he was helping her access private documents. Tony led her to the administrative offices. A muscular man with thick hair and a mole on his left cheek pointed in the direction of the Commission's filing room. He waved congenially at one of the guards pacing the hallway. When the man was out of earshot, he spoke to Tony and Afosua in a low, urgent voice.

"Right this way Mr. Coffie," he said. "I was expecting you a few minutes before now. I can only guarantee you ten more minutes without being detected. I've laid the documents on the table so you can go over them quickly."

"Thank you," said Tony. "I know this is a risk for you."

"Now we're even," replied the man. "Just leave the papers in the red file I've placed on the table when you're done. I'll be back in exactly 15 minutes to get them."

The man ducked out of the door and disappeared from view.

Afosua opened the government file cabinets and rifled through the papers. A map for the land that the Swedes had proposed use for fell out.

"Tony, look at this," she whispered. "See where the boundaries of the approved site lay?"

Tony leaned over to see she was pointing at. The light scent of her perfume and the fact that they were alone was distracting to him. His attention diverted away from the map to Afosua. However, she was so absorbed with the sheet of paper that he turned back to it, too.

"What about it?"

"The boundaries of Jurgen's map lay further toward the east, closer to the water supply. Those aren't the lands that they bid for."

Tony looked at his watch.

"We have to hurry," he cautioned. "We only have a few minutes left."

"Okay. I think there's a copy machine in the corner. I'm going make a duplicate of this."

Afosua grabbed the entire file and walked behind the white bearing wall where the machine was located. She set the map on the copier and prepared to hit the start button. A familiar voice in the room behind her stopped her cold.

"Tony! What are you doing here?"

"Oh! Mr. Boakye... so good to see you!"

The two men shook hands and exchanged formalities. Afosua slid to the ground and held her breath. She couldn't afford to be detected by Mr. Boakye, not when she had just realized what he was up to.

"What brings you to the Lands Commission?"

"I'm just checking up on some one-two one-two for a client of mine," said Tony noncommittally.

"I didn't know that accountants could be so versatile," mused Harold Boakye.

"Yes, well – it behooves me to know as much as I can about the world of finance, and that includes purchasing," replied Tony. "It increases my perspective. My knowledge in areas outside of accounting has certainly helped Phillips & Boakye, wouldn't you say?"

Afosua heard Mr. Boakye hum in agreement.

"Speaking of the firm, is anybody from the office here?" asked Mr. Boakye "I thought I saw Ms. Gymefi's car."

Tony shook his head.

"Not that I'm aware of."

"Hmm... I see."

"I have to get going," said Tony, looking at his watch. A clerk was supposed to be bringing me some files, but I don't know where he's gotten to. Want to walk out with me?"

"Sure. I have to go into the admin offices myself. I also need a file."

Afosua's heart threatened to leap out of her chest. She was holding the very file that Mr. Boakye was looking for. When the men's footsteps had become fainter, she stood to her feet and pressed the 'start' button. Nothing happened.

"Oooh ah!" she growled.

The archaic machine was unplugged. She didn't have time to wait for it to warm up. She grabbed her phone and hastily took a picture, hoping the quality would turn out okay. She placed the map back into the file and left it on the table, just as the mysterious clerk had instructed. She leaned her head out of the doorway to see if anyone was in the halls. It was all clear. Down the hall, she could hear Tony's boisterous voice weaving a tale that had all the workers laughing. He was buying her time. She walked briskly down the hall and hopped into her car. There was no time to think about how close she had come to getting caught. She had to get out of there.

****

Sophia hugged Annette in the hallway as they both prepared to re-enter the courtroom. There was nothing sexual in the gesture, but people gave both the women disapproving stares. How could someone as prominent and respected as Sophia Ike rally behind a criminal like this? Two men attempting to find seats in the audience sneered at Annette as they approached the door.

"What are you hissing at? Heh?!" growled Sophia. "Come on. Get away from here!"

Annette pulled her lover's sleeve.

"We have to stay calm," she said pleadingly.

Sophia and one of the men locked eyes in mutual distaste, until both the men had disappeared into the courtroom.

"Foolish twat," she spat.

"Sophia…Please."

Annette's pleas for civility brought her back to center.

"Look, we need to get inside anyway. We don't want to miss the show do we," she said, attempting a joke. "After all, you are the star, isn't it?"

Annette offered a weak smile and let go of Sophia's hand once they reached the door.

"I'll see you afterward?" she asked hopefully.

"Yes, of course. I'm not going anywhere."

Annette put on a brave face and walked to her seat in the front of the courtroom.

*****

"Mrs. Prah, would you say your husband has been very generous during your marriage?"

"I suppose."

"Have you ever lacked for any material things?"

"No."

"Have you been well fed? Has he ever starved you?"

"No."

"Has he ever laid a finger on you in anger? Abused you physically in any way?"

"Physically? No."

Sylvester Acquah scowled at her qualification of the question. He liked things to go according to his expectations and, more specifically, did not like to be challenged in any way. This made him a very poor lawyer.

"So Mr. Prah is a very good husband then?"

"If by your definition of 'good' you mean dressing me up like a doll and keeping me in the house, then yes – he a very good husband."

"Then why, Mrs. Prah, would you steal such an exorbitant sum of money from a man who has never let you lack for anything?" Mr. Acquah howled.

"Objection, your Honor," Lydia rumbled.

"Sustained."

"I'll rephrase my question," growled Mr. Acquah. "If Mr. Prah was such a good husband, would it seem reasonable to steal from him?'

Annette knew what he was implying, but couldn't phrase an answer to combat his meaning. She sighed when she answered.

"No."

He smiled triumphantly.

"Thank you, Mrs. Prah. No further questions."

"Ms. Oppong?" called the judge.

"Yes, my Lord," said Lydia, rising from her seat. Her robe swept around her body like a dark cloud bringing doom. She looked at Annette intently, like a mother inspecting a child's face for crumbs.

"Mrs. Prah, how would you characterize your relationship with Mr. Prah? Was he affectionate?"

"Not at all," Annette replied. "He was very controlling."

"How so?"

"Well, he limited the number of friends I could have. He never let me go anywhere unaccompanied. And he's alienated me from my family. I haven't seen my parents in 20 years."

Annette's eyes began to well up when she thought about her lost relatives. She was overcome by how much she'd missed them all this time. She had suppressed her memories of her family for so long that she wasn't sure how to handle them now. She gave in and broke into tears. Lydia handed her a handkerchief.

"Mrs. Prah, have you ever stolen anything in your life?"

"Never," said Annette vehemently.

"Never? How can you say that? Surely you've stolen something at some point. A biscuit as a child...maybe even a toffee? Perhaps you've stolen a pencil from a fellow classmate?"

"No," Annette reasserted. "My father was a kind and loving man. He never let me go without anything. He sacrificed a lot so that I could have the things that I needed, and I've known that from an early age. I never had a reason to steal – anything."

"Do you miss your father?"

Annette caught a sob in her throat.

"Very much."

Lydia turned her back to Annette, so that her voice carried over the room.

"It would be difficult for anyone to endure the separation caused by the loss of a parent. Death is difficult enough, but to know that your family is out there… not knowing how they are faring, or to share Christmases or birthdays, or to help them through illnesses that we ALL face at one time or another! Well, that has to be tortuous."

Annette nodded.

"It has been."

"And to know that this torture has been meted out by the hands of your husband, the one charged with caring for – and presumably loving you – why, it baffles the mind."

Sylvester opened his mouth to object, but was unsure whether he should do so. Lydia glanced at him and walked determinately over to the witness box where Annette was sitting.

"Have you been tortured, Mrs. Prah?"

"Yes."

"By your husband?"

"Yes…" Annette whispered.

"Objection!"

"I have no further questions, my Lord."

Lydia sat at the bar and looked around the room. She had planted a seed of doubt. She could tell by the conflicted faces of the witnesses.

"Mrs. Prah," called Judge Gyempoh. "Mrs. Prah, you may step down."

Annette's eyes were red-rimmed, but she lifted her head courageously and went back to her seat. All she could think of was her beloved hibiscus tree that Mr. Prah chopped down year after year. The image of its petals in bloom gave her comfort. No matter how hard Mr. Prah tried to kill it, it always came back thicker and fuller.

******

Afosua looked around her dimly lit home waiting for her laptop to power up. Reminders of Naa Akweley's presence filled each corner. On the kitchen counter, the sugar bowl was still half filled where Naa had left it. Afosua didn't eat white sugar; Naa Akweley wouldn't touch her tea without it. The notes that she had so dedicatedly prepared for their wellness center still sat on the table. Afosua thumbed them delicately, careful not to disturb them too much. If Naa Akweley did come back, Afosua wanted her to find everything as she had left it. She wanted to believe that her friend was happy and doing well, but in her heart she knew better. Scoundrels like Ian never change their spots: they just shift them around into new patterns.

The chime of her laptop broke Afosua's thoughts. She quickly opened the file for Jurgen's plans and uploaded the image of the map on her phone. The light above her head browned out and then brightened again.

"Please ECG, don't turn the lights off tonight!" Afosua implored the unreliable electricity supplier. It would be just like them to cut the power at a critical moment like this.

When the two files opened, Afosua compared the boundaries of them maps. The map on Jurgen's file encompassed six hectares of land, including a tributary of water off the river Volta. The approved government map did not.

"Just as I thought," she murmured. She leaned back and stared at the similar maps. Why wouldn't Jurgen have just asked the Commission to purchase this water from the beginning?

Someone was calling her name from the door.

"Afosua, its Tony, let me in!"

Afosua got up and peeked through the louvers. Tony was looking nervously around him. She threw open the door and bid him to come in quickly.

"Did anyone see you come over?"

"I don't think so," he breathed, sinking into a seat. "Could I have some water?"

"Yes, of course," she said, shaking her head at her lack of manners. She handed him a glass and brought her laptop over to where Tony was sitting.

"Have you figured out what the hell is going on Afosua?"

"I'm not entirely sure, but I'll let you in on my suspicions. I think Harold Boakye is up to something with the Swedish account… and it must be bad. He went insane when he first saw me working on it months ago."

She quickly ran down the history of the Swedish account and Mr. Boakye's odd involvement in it. She pointed to the dissimilarities in the two maps.

"See how Mr. Boakye's map encroaches on the water supply in the area? He obviously hasn't gotten government approval for the purchase but has presented it to Jurgen Gunnarsen as part of their master plan all the same. It's obviously a land grab. I just can't figure out why."

Tony nodded his head.

"Any project near the Volta River and its tributaries would require special permits. More permits mean more fees, and that cuts into corporate profit. What does Jurgen's organization do?"

"From what I can tell, some sort of medical research."

Tony shifted through the files on the table and looked at the letterhead from the Swedish account.

"The company is called GeneFor?"

"Yes."

Tony scratched his head and stood. He began pacing the room.

"GeneFor is one of the leaders in medical research in Europe. They've found cures for some of the worst pestilent diseases in recent history."

"Well that sounds great," said Afosua, relaxing with the news. "So why all the secrecy?"

"Their methods have been called into question and several of their trials have been banned and patents revoked. They haven't done much in Europe since intense investigations began, but it's been rumored that they are working in developing nations across Africa and South East Asia. No one has been able to prove anything though."

Afosua suddenly understood why.

"No one has been able to prove anything because the contracts are carried out by untouchables."

"Exactly," nodded Tony. "Men like Harold Boakye whose family has so much power and clout locally that no one would dare challenge them."

"So that's why GerFor is in Ghana? For a clinical trial?"

"Not just any clinical trial," said Tony darkly. "'GenFor' is an abbreviation for "Genetisk Forskning" – Genetic Research. They are going to isolate a portion of the population and make human lab rats out of them… probably with some false promise of free education or a meal here and there." Tony spat when the words left his mouth.

Afosua felt sick. Auntie Grace and the women of the village were in trouble. She had to do something.

"Afosua, how did you uncover Mr. Boakye? Was his name on any of the documents?"

"No," she said, shaking her head. "His name was jumbled – like in an anagram."

Tony stopped pacing and knelt on his knee in front of her. His expression was grave.

"I think you have uncovered something bigger than company fraud, something bigger than you expected. We have to be really careful from now on."

Tony left two hours later. He was going to make a few calls to see if he could get in touch with the Ghana Police's lead inspector. Before he left he put a smart phone on her kitchen counter.

"What is this?" Afosua asked incredulously.

"It's a cell phone."

"Yeah, obviously."

"I picked you up another phone for you. You'll never run out of credits again."

"You didn't have to do that," Afosua frowned.

"Nonsense. Everyone in Ghana has two or three cell phones, why should you be any different?" Tony joked. "Besides, I'll always know I can reach you. That makes you my girl, doesn't it?"

"If handing a woman a communication device makes her your 'girl,' then yes, I suppose I am."

Tony kissed her softly and smiled.

"You're welcome. I'll talk to you tomorrow, okay?"

"Sure," Afosua said, smiling back. "And thank you, for everything."

Afosua was thinking about what Tony had told her. She rubbed her arms vigorously, trying to fight a chill that wouldn't leave her. There was a rogue land dealer investing and reselling huge tracts of property in the country that had yet to be caught. His transactions netted millions of cedis for his foreign partners and usually left locals without their rightful property, robbing them acre by acre. Once the magnitude of what this person was doing reached the government, a manhunt was launched.

The problem was that there was very little to go on and the government didn't know where to begin. The trader had been very careful about covering his tracks. Tony thought Afosua had unwittingly discovered the guilty party: Harold Boakye.

Afosua had always suspected that Harold Boakye was not a nice man – a chauvinist certainly – but never a criminal! How was she going to bring her discoveries up to Mark? They were business partners and best friends. This information would crush him. She climbed into bed and pulled her bed sheets tightly around her. As she drifted off into fitful sleep, Afosua decided she would tell Mark in the morning.

******

The sun rose over the city like an enormous tangerine set ablaze. The early morning air was crisp and carried a faint scent of burning firewood. Lydia Oppong took a deep breath and almost skipped into the courtroom. Things couldn't have been going more perfectly than if she had written the script herself. The halls of the courthouse were empty except for a few cleaners and clerks filing in and out of the building. Lydia found a seat in the back of a hearing room and pulled her tablet out of her briefcase. They were not due in court for another few hours but she liked to come in early and read over case law before any trial. The solitude gave her the feeling of owning the room before anyone else came in.

"Barrister Oppong?"

Lydia looked in the direction that her name was being called from. A stocky man with reddish-brown skin stood at the end of the row she was sitting on. He was wearing a green shirt with white embroidery and black slacks. He had a black polythene bag in his left hand. Lydia's guard was immediately heightened.

"Yes?" she said cautiously.

The man moved in closer to her.

"May I join you?"

She held up her hand to stop him.

"That's close enough thank you. I can hear you perfectly fine from here."

The man nodded and set his bag on the seat closest to him.

"I represent certain people with a particular interest in the case you are defending," he began. "Certain 'facts' may come out about this case that these people would rather be left out. We wonder what incentives we might offer to leave these facts out of the view of the public."

Lydia looked over at the bag that was set unceremoniously down on the chair. She saw some notes peeking out from the edge. She lifted her lip in an unmistakable sneer.

"More than what you've got in that bag," she snarled.

"I assure you, madam, these are not cedis…"

"I don't care if they are rare red rocks from Mars!" she bellowed, jutting her neck forward in fury. "Your clients have quite a bit of nerve thinking that they can bribe me with a few dollars. Heh! What, they think because this is Ghana and I'm a woman I can be so easily bought?"

Lydia rose to her feet and balled her fist at her side.

"Get out!" she screeched. "Get out and tell that damned Mr. Prah to get ready to face me in court!"

Lydia's elevated voice was drawing a small crowd in the corridor. The man pleaded for her to calm down and listen to reason. The words caused her to growl. It was an inhuman sound, laden with pain. Seeing that his mission had failed, the strange man gathered his bag and hastened for the exit. Lydia glared at the spot where he had just stood, shaking with fury.

"What are you all looking at?" she barked at the cleaners standing in the door. "Leave me!"

Lydia sank to her seat and stared at the judge's bench. Ancient feelings washed over her. She was not that small girl anymore. She gritted her teeth and unclenched her fist.

She was not that small girl anymore.

*****

The man in the green shirt jumped into the front seat of a waiting vehicle outside.

"Did she take it?"

"No."

The woman in the back seat sighed.

"Well that's that then." She beckoned at the driver who was staring at her through the rearview mirror. "Let's go."

******

The rising sun filtered through Afosua's white lace curtains and danced on her cheek. Its warmth roused her gently. The passing of the night had made her a lot braver. Tony had assured her that everything was going to be okay, and she trusted him. Once the authorities were involved she could bow out and let them handle it, but she felt she had an obligation to tell Mark Phillips. She got out of bed and put the map and thumb drive into her purse. He was going to need to see all the proof for himself.

Street hawkers and crippled men in recycled wheelchairs surrounded her car as she approached Airport Road. Normally the entrepreneurial hustle of the people invigorated her, but today it made her feel stressed. As she drove in the direction of the office, Afosua felt her courage fail her again. She pulled over to the side of the road and got out of the car. There was a kiosk selling meat pies and drinks. She approached the small stall and asked for a pie, stalling for time. She pulled out her cell phone and checked the time. It was 9 am. Mark would be in the office by 9:30. She still had a little time to catch him just as he was walking in.

Afosua nibbled on the edge of the warm pie and started making her way back to her car. A little girl in a school uniform stumbled over to her with tears staining her face.

216

"Madam!" the child called.

Afosua stopped and spun around. The sight of the bedraggled child melted her heart. She knelt to get closer to her.

"My dear, why are you crying?" she asked sweetly.

"Please, I have lost my parents," the girl sobbed. "Our car broke down on the way to school and they sent me to sit down under a tree but I wandered off. Now they are gone!"

The girl was wailing hysterically. Afosua pulled out a handkerchief and wiped the child's face.

"Do you know your parents' number?" she asked, her voice full of concern.

When the child's chubby cheeks bobbed up and down enthusiastically Afosua felt relieved.

"Good. Let's call them then," she said, pulling out her cell phone and handing it to the little girl. "Call them and tell them where you are."

The child took the phone from Afosua and took three steps backward. Suddenly, she bolted, running away with the phone before discarding it into an open gutter. Afosua was enraged.

"Heh!" she shouted at the child who was fast disappearing from view.

Afosua sucked her teeth in fury and stumbled on something. It was a man's foot.

"Not a word, Ms. Gyemfi. Get in the car and don't say a word."

Afosua's heart dipped into her stomach. Harold Boakye had found her.

****

"Where are you taking me?"

"Just shut up and drive."

"And what direction am I actually supposed to be driving in, sir?"

Harold Boakye pulled a knife from a strap on his ankle and laid it on his lap.

"You are in no position to be cheeky, my dear girl," he said menacingly.

"I'm not being cheeky," Afosua said calmly. "I am just trying to figure out what you want."

On the outside she seemed calm and unshaken. Inwardly she was terrified. She couldn't believe she had fallen for Harold's simple trick. She kicked herself for not being more aware... somehow she had thought that if he was going to try to catch her, he might stage something more elaborate.

"Go east," he commanded. "Head for the road to Mampong."

Afosua hesitated for a moment, hoping for a miracle. Had anyone seen her get in the car with a strange man? Street hawkers and drivers passed by the parked car without giving it a second glance.

"Now!" Mr. Boakye screeched.

He was getting more agitated, and Afosua had to keep him calm. She put her car in gear and did exactly as he said. Harold Boakye snickered.

"You this woman, I'll teach you a lesson. I will teach you a very serious lesson."

Afosua didn't respond. As the road leading back to the office disappeared from view, so did her hope. There was a real possibility that she might not make it out of this alive.

*****

Lydia seemed more distracted than Annette had ever seen her. She thumbed absently at her files as Sylvester Acquah brought witness after witness to the stand to vouch for Mr. Prah's character. Lydia barely cross examined one and declined to cross three others. As each man got on the stand, Mr. Prah was beginning to look more and more like a wronged saint. Annette was sure that it was just a matter of time before her doom was sealed.

By noon the judge declared that they would adjourn for the day. After he left the bench, Annette scampered over to the bar where Lydia was still seated, staring off into the distance.

"What is going on!" she seethed.

"What?"

Lydia looked at Annette strangely. Annette was so incensed that she didn't catch the troubled look in her lawyer's eyes.

219

"Mr. Acquah is making him look like an angel, Lydia. Where is your head?"

"I'm sorry," Lydia murmured. She began absently packing up her brief case, stepping around Annette as soon as she was finished.

Annette was stunned. What was she going to do now? Was this part of Lydia's strategy? If so, it was failing abysmally. The sound of Kwame Prah's and Sylvester Acquah's boisterous laughter flooded the halls of the courtroom. In the midst of their uproarious chuckles, Annette heard Sylvester promise that the whole trial would be finished within a day if things kept going in this manner. Flushed, she ran after Lydia's retreating back.

"Lydia. Lydia!" she called desperately. "They're winning, Lydia!"

Lydia Oppong did not turn around. She found her vehicle and drove away.

******

When Lydia got home she drew her curtains and turned on the water in her bathtub. And old bottle of vodka sat in the wardrobe in her bedroom. She had not had a drink in years but she felt that one was warranted today. She slid into the scalding hot water with her glass and let it burn her skin. When the alcohol hit her throat, she felt as though she'd been scorched. She didn't care. She downed the glass and closed her eyes, letting her mind take itself where it would. It took her back thirty years.

Lydia was sitting on the veranda of Kobina Asare's house. The minister for education was not home and she was desperate to talk to him. She licked her lips nervously, wondering how he would take the news: she was pregnant and the baby was his. She was scared but certain that everything would be okay. He had told her many times as they made love how much he cared for her and how lovely she was. He would be stunned, yes, but she knew in her heart he would be supportive.

After what seemed like eons, his shiny black '73 Volvo pulled into the driveway. The watchman sprinted to close the gate behind him. Minister Asare scowled when he saw Lydia on the veranda.

"What are you doing here?" he whispered harshly.

"I – I had to come and see you," she smiled weakly. "I have some news."

"I told you never to come to my house unless I brought you." He grabbed her by the arm roughly. "What if my wife sees you?"

"And who says she hasn't seen me?" Lydia asked cheekily. "I think she and I would get along nicely. We clearly have a lot in common, seeing as we love the same man. We have similar tastes, apparently."

Kobina relaxed his grip on her arm. In the corner of his eye he noticed the watchman pretending not to watch the two of them.

"Come with me," he said. "Let's go somewhere we can talk privately."

Lydia felt herself get excited. She was completely smitten with Kobina Asare. At 38, he was one of the youngest MPs in the country. He was charismatic, charming, handsome, and had a body that made her want to do things that she never considered before. But he was also married, and that told Lydia that she could trust him… but only to a point.

As soon as they were on the road, Lydia broke the news in a breathless whisper.

"I'm pregnant."

"I know," he said gruffly.

"What? How did you know? I only just found out myself."

Kobina laughed condescendingly.

"I've impregnated enough girls to know when one is pregnant."

Lydia was hurt that he would lump her in with such a joyless lot. Still, she was different. He loved her. He had told her so.

"But aren't you excited that we're going to have a baby?" she asked hopefully.

"We are NOT going to have a baby."

"But…"

Kobina Asare stopped his car. They were in front of Lydia's dorm room. She hadn't even realized he had been driving in the direction of the campus. He pulled a wad of money from his glove compartment and a piece of paper from his wallet.

"I knew this day would come eventually, Lydia. Of course you know this changes things between us. I can't see you again after this.

"Kobina…"

"Mr. Asare, from now on. Got it?" He got out of his car and walked over to the passenger side. He opened the door and yanked her out.

"Call this number. The woman who answers will take care of everything. She knows what to do."

"What do you mean?" asked Lydia tearfully.

"What do you think I mean?" he scoffed. "She will get rid of the baby and you can continue on with your life, just as I will mine."

The MP got into his car and sparked the engine.

"There will be enough money left over after the abortion for you to buy yourself something nice – maybe a new dress or something for the next man."

Lydia caught a sob in her throat. This couldn't be happening. He was bribing her – paying her to kill their baby. She felt so cheap, so dirty. Did he think so little of her? Kobina looked into her eyes. For a moment, she thought she saw remorse. When he spoke, he was kind.

"Take care, Lydia. You really were something special."

Kobina Asare sped off, leaving Lydia in a dusty red cloud of pain. She felt like she was drowning.

She WAS drowning.

Lydia Oppong pulled herself out of the tub of water and coughed lukewarm liquid from her lungs. The offer of a bribe had nearly destroyed her before but she hadn't let it. Annette's desperate words rang in her ears.

Lydia, they're winning!

She had worked too hard to let the passions of her past get the best of her now. She got out of the tub and picked up the phone. She had some work to do.

Tony paced the floors of the chief inspector's office like a caged panther. Afosua's phone had been ringing and unanswered for hours. He was worried. Something had to be terribly wrong. The inspector leaned back in his office chair and tried to calm Tony down.

"If what you tell me is correct, she's okay," said Frederick Frimpong. "Ms. Gyemfi seems like an intelligent woman. We have a man stationed outside of Phillips & Boakye, and he says Mr. Boakye's car is still in the compound."

Tony stopped pacing.

"Has he *seen* Mr. Boakye?"

Inspector Frimpong leveled his gaze to meet Tony's, his bumbling error becoming apparent.

"Shit!" Tony cursed. "There are three different ways to get out of that office. Harold could have left through any of them hours ago!"

"Calm down, Mr. Coffie," said the inspector curtly. "We are on the case."

"We have to get out there and look for her!" he cried. "Get all your resources on this."

Frimpong shifted in his seat, but didn't rise.

"And where exactly would we start looking?"

Tony walked over to his desk and planted the palms of his hands on the scratched wooden surface. The whir of the air-condition was just loud enough to muffle the rage in his voice.

"I don't think you understand the magnitude of what is going on here," he said between gritting teeth. "Not only has your department failed to identify and catch a criminal, but your current inaction is going to be responsible for whatever happens to the one person who managed to. Now get off your incompetent ass and follow me."

Tony strode furiously towards the door and got into his car with his cell phone in hand. Mark Phillips picked up on the other end. He spoke quickly.

"Mark... it's Tony. There is a car outside of your office with a police officer in it. Get in it."

Inspector Frimpong barely had time to shut his door as Tony whipped his car onto the road. He had no time to waste.

****

The sound of Harold Boakye's breathing was maddening. Each time he exhaled, his nostrils made a whistling sound – like an ill wind running through a thin reed. Afosua had once made a cruel joke about it to a co-worker and now it was going to be the last thing she heard before she died. Mr. Boakye had already promised to kill her.

"This is all your fault, you know. If you had just listened to instructions, this would not be happening to you."

As Afosua glanced at him sideways, he caught her look.

"But what can one expect from a woman?" he spat. "As smart as you are, you are too dumb to follow simple instructions."

The car was getting hotter and hotter but Mr. Boakye refused to let her turn on the A/C. It was now long past noon and the sun shone relentlessly through the windscreen. Afosua raised her left hand to wipe sweat off her brow.

"Keep your hands on the steering wheel!" Mr. Boakye screamed. "Don't lift your hands from the steering wheel again!"

He sounded insane and Afosua was losing her cool exterior. The anticipation of what he was planning began to wear on her. Maybe if she kept him calm, she might be able to reason with him.

"Mr. Boakye…"

"Shut up, woman."

She sighed.

"I just wanted to tell you that we are nearly out of petrol." Afosua nodded towards the gas gauge.

"It doesn't matter. We are nearly there."

Afosua looked around. They had sped past a number of small villages on the road, which had all begun to look the same to her. Little boys in faded shorts played by the side of the road while women carried bundles of firewood or fruit on their heads. It would have made for an idyllic scene if not for the sheer terror Afosua felt stabbing her heart. If she could just get to her purse, she could get the phone that Tony had given her and call for help. Mr. Boakye didn't know it was in there.

Afosua looked desperately at her bag in the back seat through the rearview mirror. The act betrayed her.

"What are you looking at? Eh?"

He grabbed her purse and rifled through it. The sound of something vibrating made him pause.

"Oh!" He laughed. "Where you hoping to get to this?"

He rolled down his window and threw the phone out the side. Afosua saw it disappear from view in the grass.

"No!" she gasped.

Her protest earned her a slap. Tears of fury and despair welled up in her eyes.

"Oh. Don't worry. This will soon be over," said Mr. Boakye kindly. "Pull over here."

'Here' was in the middle of nowhere. Dense bush lined either side of the road. Soon there was nothing but the eerie sound of crows calling to each other from the lush emerald canopy. Harold Boakye pulled Afosua out of the car and pushed her into the thick foliage.

"Walk that way."

He looked absolutely deranged. The wheezing from his nose was getting louder and faster, and his bloodshot eyes were wide behind his glasses. Sun rays glinted off the cold metal blade that seemed melded to his right hand. The thought of her undiscovered body lying in the bush made Afosua tremble. She tried one last time to appeal to her captor. She opened her mouth, hoping that the next phrase she uttered would elicit some pity from him. All she could muster was a pathetic 'please.'

"Move," Harold Boakye grunted.

Mr. Boakye walked behind her, pushing her roughly in the direction he wanted her to go. As she trudged through the bushes, the rustling of wood animals as they scampered away startled her. A pair of animal eyes peered at her from the dense growth. As she got closer, they disappeared. Soon the tangled bush gave way to an overgrown path that led to a burnt out building. From a distance, Afosua made out a few details. It was a modest dwelling with about four or five rooms. To the right of it was an old covered up well.

"This was my grandfather's first building," Afosua heard her abductor say behind her. "They used to tell us stories about him. It was supposed to be a magnificent home when it was finished, surrounded by gardens and fruit trees. But as usual, a woman ruined everything."

Harold kicked at Afosua's heels as they got closer to it.

"My grandfather installed a gas stove – very modern in those days – and told my grandmother not to touch it until he could show her how to use it. But you women cannot follow simple directions! She left the switch to the tank on for too long and by the time she struck the match the air was full of gas. The explosion blew everything my grandfather had ever worked for to bits."

"But he survived... he made a new beginning," Afosua said, trying to empathize with her captor. "He left you with a legacy."

"Not before it killed him!" Harold screamed. "The toil of rebuilding everything sent him to an early grave. He never got to see the work that his sons and grandchildren did, all because of some woman who was too smart for her own good."

Harold grabbed Afosua by the arm and spun her around.

"In many ways, you and that old woman are very much alike. You think you are so smart! My grandmother should have died in that house all those years ago, but she didn't," Harold said ruefully. "But *you* will. You will not ruin everything I have worked for."

Afosua's heart was pounding like a jackhammer against her chest. She stepped backward until her feet led her to the broad wall of the old house. As her back fell flat against the crumbling concrete she let out a whimper, making Harold Boakye smile in depraved delight. Afosua looked like a small, scared creature, ready for slaughter. As her tormentor inched stealthily closer to her, Afosua wished desperately that she was back in London with her regular can of mace. Then she remembered the packet of ground pepper that Elizabeth Anaan always insisted her daughter carry. If what her mother said was true, the pepper would blind this evil man – at least temporarily. Afosua put her palm into her back pocket and felt for the little pellet.

She had to time her next move just right. As Harold Boakye raised his knife and prepared to plunge it into Afosua's heaving chest, she reached into her pocket and flung the caustic substance in his eyes. Afosua darted past Harold as he dropped to his knees and howled in pain. The terror of knowing how narrowly she had escaped death propelled her feet. When she got to the end of the grown over path, she look around in bewilderment. Which way was the road? The sun was barely visible through the lush trees. It would be dark soon, and it could be hours before another car passed this way. She jogged westward, pausing to catch her breath. She could hear her blood pounding in her ears. Afosua stopped for a moment to rest her hands on her knees and wipe a flood of sweat from her forehead. In the distance she thought she heard the rumbling of a tipper truck. She desperately made her way towards the sound.

When she got to the road, all that was left of the truck was a billow of black exhaust and fast fading brake lights in the distance. Afosua stood hapless, considering her next move. She panicked, realizing that Harold had the keys to her car in his pocket. She would have to walk to the next village. Before she could take a step, someone had grabbed her by the waist and wrestled her to the ground.

"You thought you could run away from me, you little bitch!"

Harold Boakye's bony hands pummeled her face, leaving her dazed. The pain of each blow reminded her of the night she had been attacked by Rafiq in the woods. And that's when it happened. A destructive rage that had been buried deep inside Afosua overflowed and unleashed itself on the man. Afosua grabbed Harold by the ears and pulled his head towards hers, screeching at a pitch so high that it sent roosting birds fleeing from the trees. Mr. Boakye grabbed his head in pain and tried to re-orient himself. The knife he intended to murder Afosua with lay idle next to his feet. Afosua grabbed his abandoned blade and plunged it deep into his groin.

She didn't look back as she ran away and left him gasping in the bush.

******

Mark Phillips sat in the front of the police jeep, battling the reality he was being asked to face if what Tony had told him was true. He had always known Harold to be sly and to readily succumb to his temper. He never thought him capable of kidnapping and murder, however. It might already be too late for Afosua.

When he saw a curvy woman of Afosua's build hobbling down the road, he was elated.

"There she is! Pull the car over!"

Tony had already seen her. The police jeep barely had enough time to halt before hitting his car. Tony hopped out and gathered a battered and exhausted Afosua into his arms, cradling her and gently wiping blood from her battered face.

"Tony... how did you...?"

He shushed her and helped her get to the car. Tony took out a handkerchief and wet it with water before pouring small sips into her mouth.

"The phone I gave you has a GPS app on it," he explained. He gently dabbed the corners of Afosua's mouth. "We found it on the side of the road a few miles back. I figured if we just kept driving we would eventually find you."

Afosua rested her head against Tony's broad chest and sobbed.

"I think I killed him."

"Who?"

"Mr. Boakye," she said breathlessly. "He took me out here… and I stabbed him."

"Save your strength," Tony said softly. "We're going to get you to a hospital back in Accra. You can give your statement there."

Inspector Frimpong materialized at the side of the window a few moments later.

"We've found Mr. Boakye," he stuttered. "He needs urgent medical attention. He has a knife stuck in his – that is to say – in his…"

"I think we get it Inspector," offered Tony. "I'll take the lead and meet you in Accra."

Those words and Tony's voice were the last things Afosua heard before she blacked out.

Someone was sweeping outside. The sound of stiff palm bristles and a woman's soft voice humming a hymn pulled Afosua from her sleep. The room was deathly silent, save for the distant sound of the spiritual song. That... and someone else's breathing. Afosua sat up in a panic and looked around.

"Good afternoon, beautiful," Tony whispered. "You've been asleep for a while."

Afosua put her hand on her forehead and leaned back against the pillow.

"How long have I been here?"

"Only for a day," Tony replied, pouring her a small cup of juice. She took the liquid and drank it greedily.

"You're a bit knocked up but the doctor thinks the shock of your ordeal might be worse than your physical bruises."

"By 'ordeal' do you mean kidnapping and near murder?"

Tony smiled and nodded. She seemed to be ok but he didn't want to upset Afosua by talking about what she had been through, so he fluffed her pillow and rubbed her head instead. Afosua moaned and he rubbed a little harder.

"I wish I could say that was pleasurable, but my head is killing me," she said apologetically.

"Sorry – sorry! I didn't mean to hurt you."

"I know," she smiled.

Tony was about to say something when a nurse walked in with a chart and a bottle of pain killers.

"You're awake!" she said with glee, and a little too loudly.

"Yes..."

"Ei! As for this your husband? He never left your side oohhh. I wish I had a husband to treat me so nicely. And he's very handsome too!"

The nurse smiled approvingly at Tony, making a poorly veiled attempt at seduction as she bent over to feed Afosua her medication. Afosua swallowed the pills and closed her eyes, suddenly exhausted and drowsy.

"He's not my husband," she murmured.

"Saa?" she heard the nurse marvel before she let out a girlish, flirtatious laugh. "So would..."

"No, we're not married, but I do love her," Tony said pointedly, cutting the nurse off.

Afosua smiled absently and drifted back to sleep. When she woke, Mark Phillips was standing in the corner of the room talking to Tony. She cleared her throat to get his attention. Mark grinned and sat on the edge of her bed.

"Do you think you've napped long enough?" he joked.

"I think I'm ready to get out of here. I'm not a fan of hospitals," she said frankly. "Any idea when I can be discharged?"

"By the end of the evening, if we're told correctly," Mark replied. "I wish you had told me you had such an exciting leave planned. I would have asked to join you!"

Afosua nodded and pinched at her bed sheets, forming little white peaks with her fingertips. Mark covered her hand with his.

"In all seriousness, Afosua – what you did was courageous, but very dangerous. I wish you had come and talked to me about it first."

"I know, Mark," she sighed. "But I didn't know who I could trust. I didn't know…"

Her voice trailed off.

"I understand," Mark said, filling in the silence. "But perhaps you will have the opportunity to find out that I am very trustworthy. We've just had a new position open up at Phillips & Boakye… although we'd have to seriously consider a name change, given the circumstances. Phillips & Gyemfi, perhaps?"

Afosua brightened at his words and sat up straighter.

"What? Really? You'd really consider me for partner?"

Mark laughed.

"Ah. But of course! I think you'd make a fine partner. Judging by the state of your face, I'd say there isn't anything you wouldn't do for the company."

When Afosua frowned, Mark thought he had offended her. Maybe she was more sensitive than he imagined.

"Do you think you can handle it?"

"I'm just hoping you can handle me!" she smirked.

Mark chuckled and said his goodbyes. He shook Tony's hand on the way out.

Feeling suddenly renewed, Afosua swung her feet out bed and motioned to Tony.

"Can we call the discharge nurse? I'm ready to go home now."

******

Afosua waited anxiously for Tony to bring the car around to the front of the hospital. She still wasn't sure what to make of him. Why was he being so attentive? She had done nothing but give him the cold shoulder except when she wanted something. That still hadn't been enough to drive him away. In her heart, Afosua was glad that Tony had not abandoned her, but her mind could make no sense of it at all. She was also eager to get to a phone and find out what had happened to poor Annette in the last few days. The sound of frantic shouting in the street cut into her thoughts.

"Madam! Madam! *Agoo!!*"

A dark sinewy man in a 'Made in America' t-shirt was trying to get past her. He was hurriedly carrying a lifeless woman into the entrance. A woman in traditional cloth chased after him, toting a very expensive-looking hand bag. Afosua felt really sorry for her. She doubted that the injured woman would pull through – her face looked absolutely mangled. The taxi that the woman had been brought in was still parked in front of the building. Curious, Afosua strode up to it and asked the driver what had happened. One good thing about Ghana was that everyone was eager to play reporter.

"Oh, sistah. It was so pathetic," the driver explained to Afosua, clicking his tongue remorsefully. "The woman was driving and lost control of the car. She hit a big pole and destroyed the whole car!"

The man made wide gestures and shook his hands to display the magnitude of the crash.

"Oh, I see."

"And what is even more sad, eh, is that the woman is pregnant. That is why me? I will never allow my wife to drive if she is pregnant!" he declared. "I mean how! And it was such a fine car too. A nice Nissan."

"What area did the crash happen?" Afosua asked breathlessly.

"Oh. At Dzorwulu, closer to that big church. We had to drive so far to bring her here. Luckily, some good Samaritans came to help me bring her to the hospital."

Afosua looked towards the open hospital doors and felt an acid pain in her heart. She wanted to drop to her knees, but her feet carried her back into the hospital instead. She already knew who the woman had to be.

Please God – No... not my friend.

She hoped she wrong and it was not Naa Akweley who had just been brought in. When the charge nurse confirmed that it was, Afosua lay on the ground and screamed until her voice gave out.

The bullfrogs were croaking a baleful chorus from the lush grass lining the road leading into Elmina. A sudden downpour had drenched the area. The frogs may have been singing praises of thanks for the rain, but Lydia cursed it. Although the view of the sea on the way to the Western Region was lovely, she hated the drive, especially in the rain. Ever since the road had been repaved, taxi and tro-tro drivers took over the lanes at breakneck speed, vexing her more with each passing mile. If the directions she had been given were correct, her ordeal would soon be over. She pulled her Mercedes in front of a brown and white gate adorned with a large adinkra symbol in the center.

"Mate masie. What I hear, I keep," Lydia muttered to herself. "I wonder what I'll find out inside."

She knocked on the gate and waited. Just beyond the walls someone was listening to a radio program on the topic of youth development. She wondered if the council man or woman for the area was taking notes on how to enforce these ideas. This area of Ghana looked much like the rest: underdeveloped. Lydia knocked on the gate again, more insistently this time. A teenage girl opened it up just a crack. When she saw Lydia's car and the cloth she was wearing, she knew that she was a woman of stature. She opened the gate wider.

"Madam, good evening," the girl greeted in Twi, standing aside to let Lydia into the compound.

Lydia stepped in and looked around the neat facilities. The courtyard was laid over with concrete and the walls were freshly painted white. A small sweet garden was to the left of the main door, adorned with purple and white 'ladies in a boat' and a rose bush. Another girl sat under the leafy mango tree that dominated the small lawn. This was a well-cared-for abode, not left to disrepair. There was love here… but Lydia couldn't shake the feeling that there was something forced and pretentious about it as well.

"Good evening," said Lydia, smiling at the girl kindly. "Is Mr. Fawaz in?"

"Yes Madam, he is in," she confirmed. "Please, would you like to come to the hall?"

"Yes, thank you," said Lydia. "Please go and call him for me. Tell him Barrister Oppong is here."

The hospitality in Ghana's towns and villages was unmatched, and visitors were always welcomed – expected or not. This was one thing Lydia loved about traveling outside of Accra. She settled into a brown armchair close to the door and set her briefcase by her feet. The tension in her back eased greatly. She was happy that she was no longer on the road. The girl returned with a glass and a bottle of water on a silver tray and set it on the table beside Lydia.

"Please, he said he is coming," she said softly.

"Thank you."

Lydia poured her water and took a sip. A grandfather clock ticked in the corner, reminding the occupants of its presence with every sweep of the second hand. It was imposing and too large for the room. Lydia tried to ignore it and rehearsed her speech in her head. She had gone over it again and again during the drive to Elmina. How was Annette's father going to receive her request? It was all in the presentation. She would have to be winning and convincing.

There was no more time to consider how she would say her next words. Her host entered the hall and took a seat across from her.

"I wondered when you might come, Barrister Oppong. I've been expecting you."

The half-smile on Lydia's face vanished completely once recognition of the man set in. It was the same man who had just tried to bribe her a few days ago.

"You!" Lydia gasped.

Her glass dropped from her hand and fell into her lap, spilling water all over her pale yellow and blue skirt. She struggled to compose herself.

"Who are you?" she demanded.

"I'm Jonathan Fawaz. I'm Annette's brother."

****

The quick evening shower that pattered against the hospital's clay roof woke Afosua from her sleep. She hadn't realized she'd drifted off and she sat up with a start. Tony was snoring loudly in the chair beside her. No doubt he was just as exhausted as she was, but he had refused to leave her alone.

Hospitals were such a strange place – they brought comfort and joy or pure pain and loss. Afosua wondered which she might experience that evening. Every so often a nurse would come to the waiting room and give updates on Naa Akweley's condition. Despite the advice of the staff, Afosua had refused to leave. You have just been discharged yourself, go home and get some rest, they said. There was nothing she could do by sitting here, they said.

But she could at least she do that. She could sit and she could wait.

Finally, a doctor stepped into the waiting room to talk to Afosua. She held her breath waiting for his news.

"Mrs. Blankson is stable now. She's very weak, but she's stable."

Afosua felt a tear run down her cheek. She tightened her lips to keep a cry of relief from escaping.

"She's not out of the woods yet," he continued. "She's going to need a massive blood transfusion. She lost quite a bit after we performed the emergency c-section."

"How is the baby?"

The doctor bowed his head.

"The baby will need to be transferred to Korle Bu hospital and sent to the NICU," he said gravely. Although he was full term, the impact from the car accident caused some damage as well."

"But he's alive… right?"

"Yes. He's alive, but he's in critical condition."

Afosua allowed her emotions free reign at last and let out a deep sob. The phantom pain of losing her own baby was soothed knowing that Naa's son had lived.

"We have to work on getting some blood donated," the doctor said gravely. We have a shortage... not nearly enough for all the patients who come through our doors."

"Please do everything you can for her," Afosua begged.

"Yes, we will," he smiled. "You can go in and see her now, I think. Her room is just this way."

Afosua made a beeline for the double doors beyond the charge nurse's desk. The doctor called out to her, and asked her to stop a moment.

"Do you know where we might find Mr. Blankson," he asked. "We can't tell which number is his in her cell phone and there are dozens of numbers. No one is picking up at the church either."

Afosua paused and then looked out of a window.

"No, no I can't say that I know where to find him," she lied. She walked quickly into the ward before she had to tell another.

There were four women in the pale blue and white hospital room. Afosua stepped sideways to avoid bumping into a large table that held wound dressings and other medical materials. There was a plastic pail on the floor, either to catch urine or vomit; she didn't care to know which. Afosua found her friend bandaged up in one corner of the room. She looked so small without her enormous belly now. Afosua was shocked by the sight of Naa Akweley, whose face was barely visible through the wraps. She plastered on a fake smile. Naa Akweley's breaths were deliberate and deep, as if each one would be her last. Afosua held her hand and rubbed it. Naa squeezed it back.

"You... came," she sighed.

"Yes I came," Afosua fussed. "I have never stopped thinking of you, my sister."

"You were right," Naa croaked. "Ian didn't change. Caught him... caught him in the sanctuary with the receptionist..."

"Shhh, Naa. It's alright. It's all over now."

"I tried calling you. You didn't pick up. I wanted, I wanted to come home. I came looking for you."

It was getting harder for Naa to speak now. She seemed weaker with every passing second. Afosua called for the nurse, trying to keep the alarm in her voice in check.

"I'm so sorry my friend. I'm so sorry I wasn't there when you needed me."

"Where's...baby?"

"Your baby is fine," Afosua smiled through her silent tears. "He's going to be well looked after."

Naa Akweley squeezed her hand tighter now.

"Tell everyone... everything. Ian, me, everything. Promise!" she gurgled.

"I will. I promise, Naa," Afosua whispered. "He will NOT get away with this."

The nurse slipped her stethoscope on and listened to Naa Akweley's chest.

"There's fluid filling up in her lungs," she mumbled anxiously. She turned to Afosua. "Please, I have to ask you to leave."

"But –"

"Please, if you want to help your friend, go and call for a doctor right now!"

******

"What the hell is going on here?" asked Lydia, her expression sanguine. "Where is Mr. Fawaz?"

"I am Mr. Fawaz."

"Oh don't be obtuse," Lydia snapped. "You know exactly what I mean. Where is your father?"

"He's dead," said a female voice from the darkened corridor behind Lydia. "He's been dead for four years."

The female figure emerged from the shadows and walked into the living room. Lydia was staring at Annette – or a woman who looked just like her. She had the same light eyes which also had Annette's mournful expression. The woman was a little heavier than Annette, but they were identical otherwise.

"My name is Amy. I'm Annette's twin."

"Her identical twin…" said Lydia, stating the obvious.

Amy nodded. She asked Lydia to sit down so that they could talk. As Amy sat, she arranged the sleeves of her pink and white butterfly-style boubou so that they framed her arms perfectly. She took a deep breath before she spoke.

"Grief killed my father, you know," she said softly. "When Mr. Prah came for Annette, it was hard for him to carry on normally, though God knows he tried."

Amy's attention was drawn to the shifting curtains which were fluttering in the evening breeze.

"His children were his pride and joy. He would boast to all his friends about us. He said he had the most beautiful family in the world. And when his daughter was taken away to pay off a debt – a debt he had created himself – it felt like his heart was ripped from his chest."

"But why did he not come and try and find Annette?" asked Lydia. "Why haven't any of you come to see her in all these years?"

"Part of Mr. Prah's agreement was that we never try and contact Annette," answered Jonathan. "That was the hardest part for Daddy. He was so ashamed."

"Our old house in Accra had so many memories of Annette, and my face was a daily reminder of her of course," said Amy soberly. "Eventually our parents built a house in Elmina to try and forget the past and start a new future, but they were chasing a dream."

"Or running from a ghost," Jonathan countered.

"I see," mused Lydia. A thought suddenly occurred to her. She pointed to Jonathan. "You said you were expecting me. What did you mean by that?"

Amy rose from her seat and asked Lydia to follow her.

"I want to introduce you to our mother."

The house looked deceptively small from outside. Each hallway seemed to lead to another and yet another. Lydia soon discovered that the Fawaz's home was not one unit, but three semi-detached homes connected by a small labyrinth. Amy opened the door of the most eastward wing and ushered Lydia in. There was an elderly woman lying on a daybed staring blankly at a small television. Amy introduced Lydia to the frail woman.

"Barrister Oppong, this is our mother, Esther Fawaz."

Lydia greeted the woman cordially. She did not respond.

"Our mother can't talk," explained Jonathan as he arranged her covers. "She lost her powers of speech a few months after our father died. She had a massive stroke."

"I'm sorry to hear that," Lydia said sympathetically. She really did feel for the family. They had been through quite a lot. "Did your mother hope for Annette's story to get out? Is that why you were expecting me?"

Amy shook her head.

"On the contrary, no. She never wanted the truth about Annette to come out."

"What!"

"You have to understand," Amy said quickly. "There was so much shame in what was done that my mother and father swore that they would take the truth to their graves."

"It would be a stain on our family's name if it got out," Jonathan added. "For all these years, we have done everything possible to seal the dirty Fawaz family secret. That's why I came to see you, why I brought you the money."

"Let me get this straight." Lydia spoke tersely. "You mean to tell me that you came to bribe me so that I wouldn't tell the court that your father SOLD your sister?"

Amy winced at the words and looked at her mother. Esther lay motionless until the word 'sold' was mentioned. Her eyes widened – but only slightly – as she continued to stare into distance. The movement was not missed by Lydia. She took a breath before choosing her next words.

"I want you both to hear me," she said in a more measured tone. "I am not without sympathy, but your sister is fighting to defend herself against a crime she did commit. My only allegiances are to her; not your family's 'honor.' After all she's been through, you have an obligation to help her in any way that you can. The two of you have to come to back to Accra and tell the court what you've just told me."

Amy and Jonathan looked at each other, preparing to make their pitiful objections. Lydia stopped them before they could try.

"Allow me to help you with this. Either you come with me on your own terms, or I will have the court send a bailiff to come and post a summons on your wall." She paused and stared at the hapless pair. "Now, which method do you think will give your neighbors more to gossip about?"

Lydia gripped the handle of her briefcase and turned towards the door, signaling that she was ready to leave. She hoped that the two would not call her bluff but was careful not to betray her uncertainty. A summons would take weeks to enforce – valuable time that she would rather not waste.

Jonathan looked away from his mother with such sadness in his eyes that it nearly broke Lydia. She knew that the decision was hard for him, and his inward struggle was almost palpable. Choosing between doing what is right and protecting the family image was a hard choice to make in this part of the world.

"We will meet you in court," he said softly.

He stepped by Lydia in order to show her the way out. Before she left, Lydia took a last glance in the room where the shell of Annette's mother lay. Amy was holding her hand, weeping softly. She wondered if Mr. Prah knew how many lives he had damaged… or if he even cared.

The soft chirping of fledgling swallows filled the early morning air. As if on cue, their mother returned with the spoils of her pre-dawn hunt, bringing food to satisfy their tiny, hungry bellies. With bits of mud and twigs in their beaks, Sophia had watched the swallow family meticulously build their mud nest underneath her awning months before. She hadn't the heart to take it down and destroy it, despite Idrisu's insistence. Sophia preferred the soft warbling of the swallows to an alarm clock. Annette also liked to watch the feathered family dutifully carry out the tasks that nature had prescribed for them. She was amazed at how they could adapt to any situation. They seemed so content. Watching them kept her mind off heavier issues. It was further incentive for Sophia to keep the nest intact for Annette's sake.

Sophia reached around Annette's waist and snuggled closer to her in bed. She buried her face in her curly hair, anticipating what the day held for the two of them. It was just past dawn, and they would have to get up to leave for court soon. Lydia was finally calling Sophia to testify. Annette rolled over and caught Sophia's pensive gaze.

"Are you worried about today?" she murmured.

Sophia nodded and looked away.

"I know you're taking a big risk," said Annette quietly. "It's risky for both of us if the truth comes out. I'm sure Lydia will do her best to ensure our safety."

Sophia sighed. "I hope so."

She suddenly brightened up and pulled Annette on top of her, coaxing her into a straddling position. She sat up and wrapped her arms around Annette's waist, eliminating the barrier between them with the union of their breasts. Sophia felt a surge of positivity flow through her. As the two woman sat cradling each other in the light of the rising sun, Sophia broke their intimacy with some news that she had been struggling with.

"I have to leave right after I testify, Annette," she said gravely.

"But why?"

"I'll be back! Don't worry," Sophia said assuredly. "I have to go and end things with my husband"

Annette pulled away from her and stared into her lover's eyes.

"How are you going to do that?" she asked suspiciously.

Sophia refused to give Annette any particulars.

"It's for your own safety that the less you know the better. Let's just say I'm going to prepare him a bowl of soup."

******

The courtroom was packed, almost beyond capacity. Annette felt like she was living in a terrible dream and that the entire city was there to witness each terrifying scene. She tried her best to ignore the growing rumble in the spectator seats behind her. People were begging each other to 'push small' in order to make room for one more. She didn't understand why so many strangers had such an interest in her personal life.

Annette channeled her attention to her nerves, which were beginning to fray. Lydia had informed her that her brother and sister would be appearing in court today, but for some reason she didn't want her to see them before they testified. She didn't understand why, and she ached to see the family she had been separated from for the last twenty years.

The noisy courtroom fell silent as the judge entered and was seated. Mr. Prah was smiling smugly from his seat, waving jovially at someone he recognized in the crowd. It was a reporter for the local gossip newspaper who had written about every salacious detail in the trial with inordinate specificity. Somehow, Mr. Prah managed to come out as the victim in each column.

"Does the prosecution have any new evidence?" asked Judge Gyempoh.

Sylvester Acquah rose from the bar.

"No, your honor, we believe that the evidence we entered proves Mrs. Prah's guilt. The family's accounts have not been reconciled, and this is because of the theft of funds. We shall be prepared to rest."

"Very well. Barrister Oppong, do you have any new evidence or witnesses?"

"Yes my Lord," said Lydia. "We have three witnesses to enter testimony today. The defense calls Sophia Ike to testify first."

Sophia walked into the witness box and leaned against the rail. Lydia nodded her head and began her questioning.

"Ms. Ike, what is your profession?"

"I'm a designer. I own my own label."

"And it is common knowledge that this is high end label. Have you been very successful?"

"Yes," nodded Sophia. "I would say so."

"Ms. Ike, what is your relationship with Annette Prah?"

"She started off as my client," Sophia said carefully. "Since then we have become very close."

"And in this close relationship, have you offered her certain perks?"

"What do you mean by 'perks'?"

"Have you given her special pricing, as one friend might do for another? Discounts on your bespoke designs, if you will."

Sophia nodded with understanding.

"Ah. Yes, I have. In fact, I have sometimes given her items for free."

"Did Annette Prah always come prepared to pay for the items, or did she have an expectation that they would always be free?"

"No, no," said Sophia quickly. "My garments range anywhere from ₵200 to ₵2,000. Annette always had her money in hand. I assume that the money was from her allowance."

Lydia turned her attention to the judge before she spoke.

"I will remind the court that Mrs. Prah has a monthly allowance of ₵1500, as confirmed by both parties."

She turned back to Sophia.

"Since you have such a close relationship with Mrs. Prah and can speak to her character, would it be fair to say that she probably just saved this left over money in the face of your generosity?"

"I think that is a fair assumption, yes," nodded Sophia. "Annette is very cautious and caring. I cannot see her doing what she is being accused of."

"Is there anything else you would like to share with the court about your relationship with Annette Prah," asked Lydia.

"No," whispered Sophia.

"Thank you, Ms. Ike."

"Barrister Acquah, would you care to cross?" asked Judge Gyempoh.

"Yes m'Lord," said Sylvester. He strode over to the witness box and glowered at Sophia. "Ms. Ike, do you presume to know this woman better than her husband? How can you know her when you are just her seamstress?"

Sophia did not like his tone. Something about men shouting made her lose her composure.

"What do you mean?"

"Well you say you 'know' her, but you are just friends. How can you be a better judge of character?"

"Is a friend not a better judge of character than a husband, especially one who tries to lock his wife in the house? Of course she tells me things she would never tell him!"

Sylvester Acquah stiffened at the allegation that Kwame Prah locked his wife in the house.

"You will just answer my questions, madam."

"Oh?" sneered Sophia, unleashing a sudden volatile tirade. "Well there is one question you would never think to ask me, so let me help you: I know Annette because she is my lover and we have been together for the last three years. I have loved her in ways that neither of you could ever imagine. So yes *jo*, after three years I know her VERY well – and yes, better than her old wretched husband!"

Someone sucked the air out of the courtroom.

Judge Gyempoh finally broke the shocked silence and addressed Mr. Prah's lawyer.

"Barrister Acquah if you have no further questions...?"

"No – no m'Lord."

"Ms. Ike, you are free to go."

Sophia straightened her sleeves and stepped out of the witness box with her head held aloof. Annette looked over at Kwame Prah, who was still staring at the empty witness box with his mouth agape. Annette chuckled quietly, delighting in his astonishment. Lydia had obviously enjoyed Sophia's exhibition and felt it was to their advantage. She hadn't made any attempts to stop the show. She called her next witness to the stand: Amy Fawaz.

Annette's smile gave way to a gasp as she saw her twin walk by her on the way to the witness stand. She wanted to end the proceedings and run to her, but she stayed planted in her seat. Mr. Prah whispered something to his lawyer, who nodded and waited. Lydia asked Amy to introduce herself to the court and explain her relationship to Annette.

"Ms. Fawaz, I have a written statement from you in which you give the details of how Annette came to be married to Mr. Prah."

Amy nodded.

"And in that statement, you say it was to settle a debt. How so?"

"In 1983 there was a famine in the country, and my father – our father's – business was hard hit, like many in the country. Mr. Prah knew my father and offered him a loan. He said that my father could give him a daughter to marry if he could not pay it back."

"And how old were the two of you at the time?"

"5 maybe 6 years old," said Amy. "Mr. Prah gave my father seven years to repay the loan."

"I see, and was your father able to repay the full amount?"

"No," whispered Amy.

"So what happened next," Lydia prodded.

"Father came to our room on the evening that Mr. Prah came to the house to collect his money. He said he needed our help. He said that one of us needed to go with Mr. Prah, so that he could stay out of jail and take care of the family." Amy paused, choking back a lump in her throat. "Annette said she would go. She's only 10 minutes older than me, but she always acted like it was 10 years."

She smiled wryly. "She left the following morning and we never saw her again."

"And why is that, Ms. Fawaz? Why did your family lose all contact with their daughter and sister?"

"Because of the shame," Amy sobbed.

"Did your father ever say how much the loan was for?"

"Oh yes," said Amy wiping her eyes. "It's a number we all knew well: 3,600,000 cedis...or $40,000. Daddy would stand outside in the courtyard and scream the number to God every night."

"And this shame you spoke of... is it because your father knew that what he had done was wrong?"

"Yes," nodded Amy.

She shot a disgusted look at the wrinkled old Mr. Prah.

"Nothing further."

Sylvester Acquah nearly leaped from his seat.

"Ms. Fawaz, how good of you to come."

Amy stared at him quizzically, but did not respond.

"My client said you might come here with this made up tale," he scoffed.

"I don't understand."

"Well, it's very obvious that you and your sister are very close, you being twins and all."

"We were close when we were little, yes," Amy confirmed.

"And being twins, you would do anything for your sister," Sylvester continued.

"Is Mr. Acquah planning on asking the witness a question, my Lord?" interrupted Lydia.

"Get to the point, barrister," warned the judge. "It's nearly lunch."

"Happily, your honor."

Mr. Acquah swaggered over to Amy in the witness stand.

"Show me a receipt."

"What?"

"A receipt! A bill of sale! Some proof that your father sold a child, and more importantly that my client bought one."

"I, I don't have a receipt," stammered Amy.

"Oh? And where is your father to show this proof? Did he send his child out to do his dirty work for him again?"

"He's dead!" wailed Amy.

The news jolted Annette. She had not learned of her father's passing until that moment. The look of intense grief on her face was not missed by the judge.

"Counselor, be very careful," warned Judge Gyempoh.

"Apologies m'Lord," said Sylvester hastily. He turned his attention back to Amy. "I'm afraid you've wasted your time coming here, Ms. Fawaz. I have no further questions."

Amy fled the witness stand and buried her face in her brother's shoulder. Annette felt the old pangs of sisterly protection strike her in the gut. She didn't get a chance to react further. The judge announced that they would adjourn for lunch.

"We will reconvene at two o'clock," he ordered.

Lydia gathered up her files and beamed at Annette, who was bewildered by her smile.

"Why do you look so pleased? We're sunk!"

"Oh, don't be such a defeatist," scolded Lydia. "Everything is going exceptionally well!"

"But we have no evidence," said Annette mournfully. "Mr. Acquah was right. My father is dead and we have no one to prove this ever happened."

"On the contrary, we do," Lydia winked. "We have Mr. Prah."

She gently nudged Annette in the direction of her siblings who were seated by the exit door. They looked uncomfortable, and the silence between the three was awkward. Lydia pulled Amy and Jonathan to their feet and smiled warmly.

"I know we got off to a shaky start in Elmina, but I'd like us to begin again," said Lydia. "There is an excellent chop bar close by, with the sweetest plantain you ever had. Let me treat you all to lunch. I think you three have a lot of catching up to do."

****

It seemed for Annette as though the world was in suspended animation. Nothing before these few moments with her brother and sister mattered and nothing else ever would. Annette held fast to Amy's hand for the two hours they spent at lunch, as though she feared if she let go she would lose her sister for another lifetime. It was clear Amy felt the same way. Neither of the sisters spoke, but each knew what the other was thinking. Lydia broke their reverie and announced it was time to go back into court.

"It wouldn't do to be late," she said, encouraging them to rise quickly. She gathered her enormous leather bag and her briefcase. "Not when we're so close to winning!"

"I'll see you both afterward, right?" said Annette hopefully.

"We won't leave until the trial is over," Jonathan assured her.

Annette and Lydia took the lead into the courtroom. Annette couldn't help but feel as though she was a lamb being led to the slaughter. All the 'evidence' against her seemed so convincing – and wasn't it Lydia who had told her weeks before that the practice of law was all about appearances? Right now, Annette appeared guilty. She was sure that Sophia's outburst had not helped her case either. After the shock of the admission had worn off, condemnation and judgment were sure to follow. She was now one of 'those' women – an aberration before God. Annette lowered her head as she passed a small crowd clustered around the entrance of the building.

The courtroom filled quickly once the bailiff allowed spectators in. Annette looked back and saw Jonathan and Amy seated in the center of the room. Feeling a lot more courageous because of their presence, she waved. Amy waved back with a supportive smile.

"Shouldn't you be sitting up there with Lydia?" asked a woman in large sunglasses.

"I'm sorry… who are you?" asked Amy.

"Annette, it's me, Afosua," she said as she sat next to her. Afosua was out of breath from rushing into the room. She wanted to take off her glasses, but feared that if she did the bruises on her face would alarm her friend.

Amy laughed quietly.

"Annette is in the front," she confirmed. "I'm her sister."

"Her sister!" Afosua balked. "I never knew she had a twin. Clearly we have a lot to talk about."

"All rise!" boomed the bailiff. "The Honorable Judge Gyempoh is presiding."

The judge took a sip of water before taking his seat. He pushed his glasses further up the bridge of his thin nose and looked around the room before settling his sight on Lydia.

"Barrister Oppong, I understand you have a surprise witness?"

"Yes, my Lord," confirmed Lydia. "The defense wishes to call Mr. Prah to the stand."

"The impudence!" shouted Mr. Prah. "What makes you think I would testify in her defense?"

Sylvester stood up quickly, nearly knocking over his seat.

"Your honor, it would be highly irregular for the defense to call my client as a surprise witness without…"

Lydia silenced him with a look.

"We are calling Mr. Victor Prah to the stand, not the prosecution," she quipped.

Annette raised her eyebrows in surprise. As Victor took the stand, he nodded in her direction in acknowledgement. Mr. Acquah was trying his best to calm his client who had launched into a furious missive.

"You stupid boy!" Mr. Prah was shouting. "I should have drowned you at birth! You are just as foolish as your mother!"

In the background, a collective *eiii!* rippled through the courtroom.

"Order!" thundered Judge Gyempoh. "Barrister Acquah get your client to settle down immediately!"

Sylvester's appeals for calm finally prevailed. Lydia smiled inwardly. Without knowing it, Kwame Prah had played directly into her hands and proved her assertions before she had even made them.

"Your honor, Mr. Victor Prah is serving as a surprise witness because he feared intimidation at the hands of his father," she explained. "As you have just witnessed in Mr. Prah's violent reaction, our concerns were justified. We did not want his testimony tainted by any threat."

"Thank you counselor," the judge answered, wiping his forehead. "Please proceed."

Lydia took three long strides and stepped in front of Victor.

"Mr. Prah, I contacted you some time ago to ask you to gather evidence to help my client. Can you tell the court what you were able to find?"

Victor cleared his throat and leaned against the wooden bar. He was 40 years old but he was shaking like a school boy.

"Yes. Well, I am a junior financial clerk at my father's – that is, Mr. Kwame Prah's – logistics company. I have worked there for 15 years in the same position. During that time, I have inherited records and ledgers from the senior clerks, some stretching as far back as the 70s."

"Carry on," urged Lydia.

"Yes. Well, in those records, I discovered several incongruities. After a certain period in time, the accounts never really balanced. This is normal in accounting, however. It is expected that there will be an acceptable amount of imbalance, give or take a few digits."

"Mr. Prah, I asked you to look into outgoing numbers within a certain time frame. Can you tell the court what those years were?"

"Yes," nodded Victor. He picked up a printed spread sheet. "They were from 1983-1985."

"The same span of time that Mr. Prah made a loan to Mr. Fawaz," Lydia said matter-of-factly. "Was there a lump sum of money that was outgoing in the year 1983?"

"Yes, there was."

"What was that amount?"

"40,000 US dollars," said Victor.

The courtroom was rumbling. Kwame Prah was slumped over in his seat. He looked as though he was struggling to breathe. Annette wanted to feel sorry for him but she couldn't muster the sympathy. His cruelty had left her breathless so many times. If he fell over and died right now, she would be the happiest widow in Accra. Lydia passed a copy of the ledger to the judge and Mr. Acquah.

"$40,000," repeated Lydia. "The same amount of money Mr. Fawaz received from Kwame Prah as a loan. The very same amount that he failed to pay back. The very same $40,000 that Annette Fawaz's life served as surety for."

Lydia stood imposingly in front of Mr. Prah at his seat. Her voice rang loud and clear throughout the courtroom.

"Ladies and gentlemen, the prosecution has failed to show beyond reasonable doubt that Annette Prah stole any amount of money. What we have seen is that Mr. Prah has a history of forgery and poor record-keeping, and accountability for those losses cannot be placed confidently at the feet of Annette Prah. What we do know now for sure is that Annette was forced into this relationship before she was old enough to give her consent. A child under 16 in this country is not considered a consenting adult, let alone a 7 year old girl."

Lydia paused, saying her next words slowly and deliberately.

"What we do know, is that Kwame Prah selected and groomed Annette when she was a little girl for his pleasure, under the pretenses of marriage – a condition he has kept her in until today. This is a clear violation of her human rights, and Mr. Prah will face the full rigors of the law for it. The tables have been turned, and Mr. Prah's reckoning is sure to come."

Lydia took her seat and left Victor seated in the witness box. Sylvester seized the opportunity to question him without prompting.

"Mr. Prah, I believe you have a confidentiality agreement that forbids you from discussing company finances with anyone outside of the shareholders."

"Yes. Barrister Oppong assured me that jurisdiction of the court provides an exception for this."

"Why are you doing this?" asked Sylvester suspiciously. "Is it because you yourself were in love with your step-mother?"

Victor smiled condescendingly.

"Mr. Acquah, you've been our family's lawyer for a long time. You know that those were my feelings as a secondary school boy. I am married with my own family now. So, no, this has nothing to do with romantic feelings for my father's wife."

Sylvester was grasping at straws. He needed to show Mr. Prah as a sympathetic figure, and he needed Victor to help him do that.

"Victor," he said intently. "Do you not see what you are doing is killing your father?"

Victor looked at the elder Mr. Prah, heaving in his seat and clutching his chest.

"I cannot say that anything I have done or said is killing him," he said quietly. "What he did was wrong, and it is up to me to do what is right."

The judge dismissed him from the stand when Sylvester said he had no further questions.

"Your Honor, could we have a side bar?" said Sylvester Acquah.

Sylvester Acquah's concern was obvious. He knew he had lost the trial. Lydia suspected he was going to try and save his client. This was the part she always looked forward to. She rose and met the men at the judge's bench. When Sylvester Acquah's voice rose into a high whine, the magistrate addressed the bailiff.

"We will convene in my chambers," said Judge Gyempoh.

"All rise!" thundered the broad chested court servant.

Lydia signaled for Annette to join her and Sylvester did the same for Kwame Prah. As the party entered the judge's dark chambers, Annette wondered what fate awaited her and the man who had shaped her life for as long as she could remember. Mr. Prah looked at her with sorrowful and pleading eyes. She knew that look well. It was the look of a man begging to be saved. She wanted to claw his eyes out and crush them with her heels.

"Not guilty!" Afosua said jubilantly, hugging her friend tightly. "I told you you were in good hands with Lydia."

She winked at her former boss and took a glass of champagne from Tony as he took a seat next to her. It was Lydia's custom to invite clients back to her house after successful litigation. It was the only time they were welcome.

"And don't forget the best part," said Lydia. "Marriage annulled and restitution in the amount of ₵20 million! 1 million for every year Annette spent locked up with that scoundrel."

Annette was too stunned to believe her good fortune. She looked around the room at her friends and family as they relived each troubled and triumphant moment in court. It was the happiest she had been in years. She wished Sophia was here to share this joy with her, but she was already in Nigeria. She wouldn't be back for a few days.

"Tell us what happened inside the judge's chambers," begged Amy.

Lydia smirked, happy to retell the most enticing moments.

"Well, Mr. Prah knew that he was facing the possibility of a long prison term, given that charges of child trafficking were in the works," Lydia said drunkenly. " 'Please have mercy on me!' he croaked 'I won't last a day in prison.'"

She stopped talking and burst into a fit of giggles.

"Annette, tell them what happened next oooo! Tell them what Judge Gyempoh said."

Annette blushed.

"He said that he had pity on me because I was now depraved, it was Mr. Prah who was to blame for damaging me, as evident..."

"As evidenced by the fact that she had become a lesbian!" Lydia giggled. She suddenly stopped laughing. "But no, seriously. Sleeping with such an old man would make me want to love a woman too. Annette was kinder than I would have been. I would have let the bastard rot in jail AND take his money, but she allowed the judge to show mercy."

Afosua knew where this was heading. Lydia had never been able to hold her drink. Pretty soon she would be dancing on every table in the room and naming names from past trials. She ushered the protesting lawyer to a sofa in a connecting room and brought her some food to absorb some of the alcohol. If she was busy chewing, she couldn't talk.

"So what are you going to do now that you are a rich woman?" asked Tony.

Annette smiled broadly.

"I'm going to live the life of my dreams." She took her brother and sister by the hand and squeezed them tightly. "I'm going to spend every day with the people I love."

Afosua walked back in as Annette was making her declaration and slipped her arm around Tony's waist. She stood on her toes so that she could whisper in his ear. He turned so that he could hear her better, accidentally brushing their lips together. She beamed and searched his eyes with hers.

"We should try that. I think that sounds like a perfect idea."

Epilogue

Afosua stood on the dock of the river basin, keeping a watchful eye over the toddler playing in the clear water. He looked so content and totally captivated by an army of tiny brown river snails making their way through the sticky mud. Tony joined her on the dock, emerging from the glass doors of the health spa. The first guests were scheduled to arrive in half an hour. He wrapped his arms around her waist and kissed her on the back of the neck. She leaned back and welcomed his embrace.

It had been two years since Naa Akweley's accident and Tony and Afosua had promised to help raise her son. They had done their best to make sure that he knew he was loved.

"The building looks beautiful," Tony said with admiration. "I think it's going to be a huge success."

"Thanks," Afosua whispered. "All the plans were Naa's. I figured it was the best way to honor her, after everything that that happened between her and Ian."

"You did the right thing," he said approvingly.

"I couldn't have done it without Annette's capital – at least not as quickly..."

"Do you ever have regrets about leaving Mark?" asked Tony. "You could have earned a good living as his partner."

"I could have," Afosua admitted, "but I don't think I would've been happy. Certainly not as happy as I am with you and the baby."

Tony looked at his watch.

"Speaking of the baby, he should probably get inside for a bath before the guests come."

"I'll take care of that," said the spa manager. She had just joined the two on the dock. She lifted her veil and called for the playing child.

"Ian! Come to Momma. Let's go and have a bath."

19818154R00147

Made in the USA
Charleston, SC
13 June 2013